The facts about the training path to Sotapanna

Volume 1

Chennai • Bangalore

CLEVER FOX PUBLISHING
Chennai, India

Published by CLEVER FOX PUBLISHING 2026

ISBN: 978-93-7500-708-1

Homage to the Supremely Enlightened Buddha!

Certainly, Buddha's Dhamma leads to four-fold nibbana.
Buddha is certainly the knower of all worlds, the highest
Jewel, the teacher of all perfected ones.
Homage to the supremely enlightened Buddha!

-Dr Ariyathushel Arahant

The gift of nibbana across stages is an excellent gift, and you may share the noble right view with anyone seeking Buddha's Dhamma freely!

Preface

The training path to Sotapanna includes multiple aspects that an ordinary person can train the mind, both through conscious efforts and nature's way. When you understand something, you can continue and grow in your understanding. This book explains and clarifies how you can understand, develop, and grow in noble understanding by letting go of the deluded or limited conventional understanding of self-view, social practices, and doubts, and by understanding the universally applicable Triple Gem, commonly known as the right view, towards Sotapanna.

Table of Contents

Introduction
Path to Sotapanna

The purpose of following Buddha's path is to end suffering with stability. The path to Sotapanna is a journey of discovering universal truths through questioning and personal investigation. By applying wisdom, you seek to uncover these answers and gain deeper insight into reality. As you are trying to investigate universal truths, you are trying to understand certain truths that are common to all human beings, not merely to a category of people. Also, investigating universal truths means adopting an evidence-based approach, in which you come to understand them through evidence within you. Given that the world is created within you, and you are part of the universe, you are attempting to understand the universal truths within you, the core, not the surface matters.

Typically, an average person is encouraged to prioritize social practices so that one may even forget that one is part of the universe. What you need to remind yourself is that the world is created within, the universe is within you. When you engage in intentional acts, as you interact with universal rhythm within and universal energies, you generate fuel within. When you engage in intentional actions based on delusion, you generate fuel again and again as you continue to grasp or interact with universal energies in an unwholesome manner within you. Depending on the kind of fuel you generate in your mental continuum, as energy transforms, fuel that burns within your mental continuum has the potential to make you experience various births or samsara. When you remain free from inner fires, they can't sustain long enough to experience further births. Matters related to how energy transformation happens within you are things you need to understand after you experience the upper stages of “nibbana” or “nirvana”. You may initially focus on training the mind to experience lower stages of nibbana.

Universal rhythms, ups and downs of life experience can make you experience shock and too much distress when you don’t realize they are a part of life. To see truths, you need to develop truths within, as much as actively engaging in letting go of foolishness, delusion, or unwise thinking patterns that contradict life experience.

Since birth, an ordinary person tends to think of the self as stable, but life experiences suggest the self is not stable. Thus, if you were to maintain the underlying tendency to think that the self is stable, that’s an illusion. If you do not maintain the underlying tendency to think that it is stable, that’s awakening to true life experience and matters related to understanding universal truths.

How do you escape sufferings coming in an ordinary mind and develop the path to Sotapanna?

By letting go of self-view to begin with. In other words, understanding worldly experience with wisdom, you can escape suffering. The only thing a person needs to be able to retain that understanding 24/7, 365 days a year, naturally, without any conscious effort because consciousness is subject to change. That's what experiencing four stages of nibbana would indicate for each person, although there are differences in understanding across stages.

Understanding impermanence at lower stages of nibbana makes one experience the best worldly experiences arising from sensory information, including sensual pleasures. Upper stages make one experience the best worldly experiences arising from sensory information, free from delusion in pursuit of sensual pleasures. When you are a Sotapanna, you will naturally have an understanding of impermanence with wisdom in your thoughts. Until then, you may make conscious efforts to avoid touching the world in an unwholesome manner in your mind, while reflecting noble wisdom and noble qualities in the universal Triple Gem, in your mental continuum.

Just as ordinary bodies function in the same universal rhythm (birth, infancy and childhood, youth, middle and old age, and likewise), ordinary mind functions in the same universal rhythm, so the mind tends to have a deluded understanding; underlying tendencies to think that the self is stable in their mental continuum. There are no changes, or no significant changes, happening in the ordinary bodies as they experience nibbana through Buddhahood or Arahantship. Instead, the significant changes that occur are the transformation of the mind states of those who have ordinary bodies through Buddhahood or Arahantship. It's useful to maintain patience as nibbana is a progressive process.

> "Not to hurt, to cultivate merit and wholesome, to purify one's mind from grasping the fetters, this is the Teaching of the Buddhas.
>
> "The best moral practice is patience and self-restraint based on the noble view; said the Buddhas."-Dhp 183,184

How do you escape sufferings coming in an ordinary mind?

To begin with, applying wisdom to experience freedom from conventional understanding of self and social practices is the way to escape the universal rhythm of the ordinary mind, or the path to Sotapanna. To get there, you may initially train the mind to function oppositely to ordinary rhythm. When things make you sad, upset, depressed, anxious, jealous, and hateful, and so on, try to first understand your mind state. After you understand your mind state, apply wisdom to transform mind states. For example, try not to be too sad when you lose things, understanding that it's not wise to let your happiness depend on them. That's because whenever the source of happiness changes, your happiness is likely to change or be affected. Also, continue working on your goals and resolve any issues that need to be addressed. In this way, you engage in wise action by reducing delusion.

How do you expand your happiness and peace beyond dependent-originated happiness?

By understanding that dependence is limited happiness, losing things is part of life (awaken to truth), as long as you have done your best to resolve things to your best, find peace in that, instead of chasing around things that are beyond your control, as it's unwise. What is unwise is what is ordinary. Then, if you can take it to the next level, try to be happy when you experience losses, as it allows you an opportunity to train to let go of dependent happiness. To expand your wisdom, you may also incorporate nature's way into your conscious effort, enabling you to associate with the universally applicable Triple Gem in your thoughts and mental continuum.

Chapter 1
Beyond the surface

It is important to understand that when you seek universal truths, you are attempting to discover truths that are not merely visible on the surface but lie beyond it, broadening your vision. Noble view, or commonly known as right view in the noble path, is about broadening the vision or widening your understanding of the universe within you with wisdom.

On the surface, you may look stable, but beneath the surface (deep truth), what a person thinks of themselves is subject to change. On the surface, people can appear nice, but inside they can harbor delusions and likes or dislikes to varying degrees. Sometimes, a person can make a display of treating everyone as precious but not actually think (or intentional action) they are worthy with stability in their mental continuum, and it can be a barrier to developing the path because, given the universe within each person, the universe knows what's in their thoughts regardless of how a person chooses to display it.

The universe is within you, and it knows what's within. It produces mirror-like consequences in line with universal laws. On the surface, when you take social practices, it appears that social practices are the right things as accepted by the majority.

Yet if you were to look at social practices on beneath, you would understand that they are unkind and mistreat people in many ways. If someone were to merely follow social practices, that's not enough, not even close to becoming a Sotapanna, as one needs to consider every being as precious to let go of fuel that makes you fire up within you when one experiences delusion. instead, social practices are designed to treat most beings as unworthy or "garbage" without preserving the dignity of a being. The world is created within you. The universal way of functioning is to generate mirror-like images of the outside within you, more like a cosmic illusion within you. Thus, if you want to let go of a distressing experience, given that a distressing experience as a consequence is produced based on what is within, you may give up root cause of the distressing experience or delusion[1]. Similarly, if you want to meet the Triple Gem, you may develop mirror-like Triple Gem within you.

The underlying tendency of an untrained mind is that at times, it can pretend to be something it's not (i.e., pretend to be kind but inside may not be that kind, or pretend to have experienced nibbana from outside but may not be able to explain things that are directly related to the four stages and the practice and likewise), for various reasons. Yet then the fuel generator within will not stop, and as a consequence, suffering

---

[1] Delusion: not understanding worldly experiences with wisdom with regard to self, social practices, and doubts regarding the Triple Gem within.

based on delusion and samsara will continue, and peace and happiness throughout the truths in the universe; nibbana will be far shore. Thus, an ordinary person may observe thoughts with extra care and let go of unwholesome thoughts within.

A common way is the underlying tendency of a person to think that everything they like should happen (i.e., expectations are grounded in a deluded understanding of self). A common way is the underlying tendency of a person to think that following social practices is an important thing and have doubts about the truths in the universal Triple Gem. Renouncing means letting go of deluded underlying tendencies based on true life experience and wisdom. Every time you touch upon your thoughts in an unwholesome manner based on common ways, it generates fuel in line with universal laws. Self knows best about thoughts, and given that the universe is within you, the universe also knows best about each person and produces consequences in line with universal laws. An untrained mind has a tendency to generate fuel again and again by understanding thoughts in an unwholesome manner, grounded in delusion. You may want to try to avoid generating fuel within, as you need to discover the truth of letting go of fuel within or the universal truths that you need to grow within, synthesizing you and the universe, balancing the mind, and purifying unwholesome thoughts by cutting the root.

When ordinary people share ordinary views, both the sayer and the listener develop ordinary views without being able to develop the noble path. On the contrary, when noble views are shared among friends by those who experience nibbana across stages, noble views can be developed, opening the noble path that is there. Learn and know how to practice nibbana precisely; practice Dhamma within regular activities. As you engage in your usual activities, you are less likely to actively focus on your mind, and chances are, your natural mind will surface. When you understand your thoughts and mind as they occur naturally with wisdom, that is how you can understand you mind without seeking or without refusing, meaning closing sensory information (closing eyes, ears etc.) but merely understanding your worldly experience with wisdom. If someone were to look at the surface, and don't understand Dhamma in depth; for them, suffering is continuously experienced in the mind, as the noble path and Buddhhood are far away. Instead, you may develop wisdom with patience and apply wisdom to investigate the depth of universal Dhamma.

Lifestyle based on rituals can still make you suffer if you have the delusion about yourself and your worldly experiences coming from sensory information. By understanding what the noble path is, if you are seeking a way out of mental distress, you may try to test the practice within you.

One obstacle to developing the universal noble path is that sometimes people give up certain things physically while retaining delusion for self, or even attachment to Dhamma or delusion toward Sangha, based on rituals. Some people may say they have practiced Dhamma for many years, meditated, or become a monk or the head of a monastic setting, and likewise, but if their mind tends to take pride in what they construct with words, they experience conceit. Even if someone happen to experiences random thoughts in which they consider themselves great, similar, or worse, and likewise, that is a mind state grasping the self-view. The noble path that leads to freedom from mental constructions requires you to work on reducing conceit from early on and letting go of the deluded understanding of self-based on conventions. When the path to Sotapanna is shared, if you were to pay too much attention to the Dhamma share's conventional background, as you grasp conventions, you are developing delusion. Delusion toward worldly experiences can delay or prevent nibbana. Instead, if you pay more attention to subject matter, whether or not a person explains nibbana as explained by the Buddha, it is how you develop confirmed confidence in the universal Triple Gem in the middle way. In addition, if you were to expect too much from your Dhamma practice, such expectations can make your delusion and attachment to yourself grow. Instead, you may give priority to the noble Dhamma practice, without focusing too much on outcomes. As you prioritize maintaining Dhamma within, the consequence will be that you will experience universal Dhamma; freedom from self and other fetters within you.

> "These are the two assemblies. The better of these two assemblies is the assembly that experiences fourfold nibbana, not the assembly that merely talks about things that are not directly related to experiencing nibbana or fancy talk…"- AN 2.47

> "Friends, by memorizing the discourses incorrectly, taking only a semblance of the phrasing without understanding the interpretation in line with four stages of nibbana, some spiritual friends shut out the meaning and fall off the teaching. They act for the detriment and suffering of the people. But by understanding the Dhamma well in line with four stages of nibbana, not taking only a semblance of the phrasing but understanding Dhamma accurately with reference to four-fold nibbana, noble people reinforce the meaning and the teaching. They act for the welfare and happiness of the people, for the people, for the benefit, welfare, and happiness of gods and humans. They brim with much merit and make the true teaching continue…"- AN 2.41

If someone says living alone means living without anyone, either in a forest, mountain, or under a shelter, physically, that's not living alone in noble path. Living alone in the noble path means not having delusions regarding the worldly experiences.

> "A person living in this way — even if he frequents isolated forest & wilderness dwellings, with an unpopulated atmosphere, lying far from humanity,

> appropriate for seclusion — is still said to be living with a companion. Why is that? Because the craving based on delusion that is his companion has not been abandoned by him. Thus he is said to be a person living with a companion.
>
> "Now, there are forms cognizable via the eye — agreeable, pleasing, charming, endearing, fostering desire, enticing — and having given up delusion, cutting off the root, a person does not relish them, welcome them, or remain fastened to them. As he doesn't relish them, welcome them, or remain fastened to them, delight ceases. There being no delight, he is not impassioned. Being not impassioned, he is not fettered. A person disjoined from the fetter of delight in mind by cutting the root or delusion is said to be a person living alone."- Migajala Sutta, SN 35.63

If someone says one has to give up physically, that is giving up certain things physically, but not giving up based on the noble path, which is delusions regarding physical things, including worldly experiences. If someone shares things that are not directly relevant to experiencing the nibbana, or explains the Dhamma loosely or incorrectly, that is not a representation of the Buddha. If someone shares things that are directly relevant to experiencing nibbana, explain Dhamma precisely; that is a presentation of the Buddha. When someone experiences the universal truth that is bigger than social truth, they don't explain that Dhamma or Sangha can be created through rituals or social practices; instead, they explain the role of wisdom and karma across samsara. Thus, when one takes a conventional monk as a noble monk, it is likely that one assumes that nibbana is a one-life time practice based on rituals, but that contradicts Buddha's nibbana. It is a practice across samsara; this explains why, sometimes, a Sotapanna can take 7 births to become an Arahant. Then, if someone were to say, "But we can't see our previous births." Then the answer would be as long as you are attached or limited to self-view, and sensory information, you are restricted, which makes you unable to surpass beyond self (and time), but if you were to let go of limitations, you will likely know it yourself as you develop triple knowledge and more when you progress across the stages of nibbana. In any case, regarding triple knowledge and beyond, this should be discussed only after a person has experienced at least the first two stages of nibbana, as the later stages follow. Thus, for those who seek nibbana, what is relevant for you at this stage is how to train for the Sotapanna experience. You may develop the noble view by letting go of deluded understanding of self, social practices to begin with, while engaging in wholesome deeds. In other words, you may live the best of each moment by applying wisdom, you may fulfil responsibilities for self and others, avoid hurting oneself and others (i.e., do not treat people differently based on social practices, etc.), maintain integrity by giving up pretending, engage in usual activities actively while putting conscious efforts to maintain the right view during waking hours and associating with the universal Triple Gem.

Chapter 2
Discovery

With the loss of true Dhamma over time since Buddha's parinirvana, an average person of modern day tends to think Buddha's Dhamma is a religion. Religion is where questions are typically not asked but merely accepted without question, and where society divides certain people as better than others, and likewise. Universal truth is hidden, and to seek truth, one requires questioning as well as seeking with wisdom, and it's the practice in which comparisons are given up. What allows you to let go of delusion, the root cause of suffering, is where the universal truth of the universal Buddha is found. By understanding the universal nature of the self and worldly experiences with wisdom, a person can let go of suffering across four stages in a stable manner. Seeking universally applicable noble truths or four-fold nibbana as an experience requires asking wise questions and seeking answers, just as you would when investigating using modern science; below are some relevant questions and answers.

How do you escape sufferings coming in an ordinary mind or develop the path to Sotapanna?

Applying wisdom to experience freedom from conventional understanding of self and social practices is the way to escape the universal rhythm of the ordinary mind, to begin with, or the path to Sotapanna. To get there, you may initially train the mind to function oppositely to ordinary rhythm; when things make you sad (upset, depressed, anxious, jealous, hateful, conceited, and like), understand your mind state, and try to transform mind states by applying wisdom while doing usual things through conscious efforts. For example, try not to be too much sad when you lose things, understanding it's not wise that your happiness depends on such things because every time the changes happen in the source of happiness, your happiness is likely to change or affected.

How do you expand your happiness and peace beyond dependent-originated happiness? By understanding that dependence is limited happiness, losing things is part of life (awaken to truth), as long as you have done your best to resolve things to your best, find peace in that, instead of chasing around things that are not beyond your control, as it's unwise, what is unwise is what is ordinary. Then, if you can take it to the next level, try to be happy when you experience losses, as it allows you an opportunity to train to let go of dependent happiness, while continuing to work on your goals and resolving any issues that need to be addressed (i.e., wise action without delusion). To expand your wisdom, you may also include nature's way into your conscious effort, enabling association with the universal Triple Gem in your thoughts and mental continuum.

Also, understand what the obstacles are for developing the noble path. One of the obstacles for developing the universal noble path is that sometimes people give up certain things physically while retain attachment to Dhamma based on delusion for self or Sangha based on rituals. Thus, sometimes, as some people say, they have practiced Dhamma for many years, meditated, or become a monk or the head of a monastic setting, and likewise, if their mind tends to experience pride over what they construct with words, that is a mind state with conceit. Even if someone happen to experiences random thoughts in which they consider themselves great, similar, or worse, and likewise, that is a mind state grasping the self-view. Therefore, to let go of fuel within, ensure to check on your mind constantly. The noble path that leads to freedom from mental constructions requires you to work on reducing conceit from early on.

When the path to Sotapanna is shared, if you were to pay too much attention to the Dhamma share's conventional background, as you are grasping conventions, you are developing delusion, and delusion to worldly experiences can delay or prevent nibbana. Instead, if you pay more attention to subject matter, whether or not a person explains nibbana as explained by the Buddha, it is how you develop confirmed confidence in the universal Triple Gem in the middle way. If you were to expect too much from your Dhamma practice, such expectations can make your delusion and attachment to yourself grow. Instead, you may give priority to the noble Dhamma practice, without focusing too much on outcomes. As you prioritize maintaining Dhamma within, the consequence will be that you will experience Dhamma; freedom from self and other fetters within you.

Chapter 3
Noble understanding or the right view

The noble path is about experiencing freedom from worldly experiences coming from sensory information with wisdom. Self, others, and the world are a mental construction. Understanding of self is a mental construction based on conventions. Understanding the self is a subjective process. The same person can be understood differently by a person and an outsider.

A person can only understand another person through one's own self; when someone says something, the same thing can be understood in various ways by another.

Noble understanding or right view is found within those who experience at least the mind state of Sotapanna. Noble understanding can be shared with others, helping them enhance their current understanding.

Chapter 4
Emptiness & Words

Words are inherently empty, but how you understand words makes them alive or meaningful for you. Words can only be read, interpreted and understood by each person's mind. The way each person understands words can differ depending on what the words mean and the subjectivity or perception of the word. The middle way means using words in a way that benefits self and others and avoids harm to yourself and others, as an aspect of Dhamma includes not hurting or harming anyone. Misinterpreting Dhamma is what is harmful, as it prevents the vision of a Sotapanna. Accurately explaining the four stages of nibbana is beneficial, as it allows those who are wise to develop noble vision. Thus, those who struggle to comprehend nature's freedom order: Arahant, Anagami, Sakadagami, Sotapanna; they struggle to progress on the noble path.

Nibbana becomes understandable to those with a high degree of wisdom, regardless of their wealth, health, education, or social identities. When someone gets an opportunity to hear a universally applicable path to Sotapanna, they hear that Sotapanna and other stages occur at random times. Sotapanna is a natural happening beyond social identities. Thus, those who struggle to comprehend the role of karma and universal laws would find it difficult to renounce and grow in understanding beyond social practices. Sotapanna, or the first stage of universal Dhamma, is something one must feel worthy to follow in one's heart, regardless of what others say, as sometimes even within the same family, among friends, or in the community that's socially seen as belonging together, one person can experience nibbana while another does not. Given the diversity of karma and wisdom, when seeking nibbana, you may have to rely on your heart; if it's calling you to the superior wisdom-based path, you may come and test the practice.

What is the practice?

Recalling the infinite wisdom and infinite noble qualities of the Universal Buddha, giving up grasping self-view, social practices is the practice leading to Sotapanna. The universe operates according to a set of fundamental rules, and there is a systematic order to how universes function. To experience cessation throughout the universe, you may understand the rules and order. When you reflect on the universal Buddha, universal Dhamma, and universal Sangha in order, and engage in letting go of self-view and social practices, that's a helpful practice to experience Sotapanna.

If you continue training as much as possible within the waking hours, 24/7 a day, and this is how you begin the path to find a refuge in yourself or Sotapanna.

You seek something because you lack it, and as you develop wholesome within, you will find yourself a place where you can find refuge across the stages of nibbana as the Triple Gem comes to develop within. To get there, one needs to purify one's deluded thinking in the mental continuum.

Self-view: You can overcome delusional understanding of self by comprehending impermanence and consistently applying this understanding with wisdom in daily life.

Social practices: You can let go the delusion associated with social practices by recognizing that societies operate within universal laws and are subject to universal functioning. Societies often lack kindness and do not embody nobility. By discerning this reality, you may choose to act beyond societal standards. For instance, while societies may favor certain groups over others, you can regard all beings as valuable and integrate this perspective into your daily actions.

Doubts: If you have doubts about the universal Buddha and Dhamma, it is because you have not yet understood them within yourself. A person can only understand within themselves. If you let go of the illusion that your expectations should always come true and realize that sometimes they do and sometimes they do not, based on life experience, that is letting go of delusion. Even if you understand this for a moment, your suffering will be reduced; during the time your understanding lasts, your doubt about Buddha's Dhamma and Buddha should vanish based on evidence within you.

If you let go of thoughts that generate inner fires, such as jealousy, ill will, pride, and the need to compare people, even for a moment, you will experience peace. Your suffering will be reduced; during the time your understanding remains, your doubt about Buddha's Dhamma and Buddha should vanish based on evidence within you.

Whoever explains Buddha's universal Dhamma beyond self-view and conventions and declares their understanding, if you test the practices they describe, you will see a reduction in delusion, even for a moment. If you understand these matters related to thoughts that generate inner fires and renounce such thoughts with wisdom, and if you sustain this renouncing through effort, you will experience reduced suffering in your mind.

If you give priority to Dhamma, for it allows suffering to go away, and to the teacher of universal Dhamma; universal Buddha, for gifting such a perfect universal Dhamma for all, and to those who reveal things that are directly related to experiencing Sotapanna because you prioritise letting go of suffering for you, you come closer to developing the noble path and the Triple Gem within, and in doing so, experience Sotapanna within. Thus, try to treat letting go of pain[2] for yourself as precious, something that is the most valuable thing for you, and begin to understand the universal path. You will tend to be fully committed wholeheartedly to something that you consider the most precious. Thus, as you consider letting go of pain as precious, it will aid you in actually applying wisdom to let go of pain coming from day-to-day experiences. On the contrary, when you begin something half-heartedly, you are more likely to drop off the path due to a lack of full commitment. By understanding what's most beneficial for you, you may make a wise choice.

[2] Pain refers to pain coming from day-to-day life experiences.

Chapter 5
Freedom from mental model

The common way of thinking and understanding self and world follows a standard mode. Escaping the standard mode with wisdom is the path to Sotapanna.

When it comes to training on the noble path, we are discussing the mind's underlying tendencies. Underlying tendencies of a mind can be hidden at times and surface at other times. Underlying tendencies can be suppressed through precepts or rules, and you already know about precepts and rules. What you need to discover is how to be free from the mind's underlying tendencies with stability in your mental continuum. Freedom from underlying tendencies, precepts, and rules is what we develop through the Sotapanna path.

Typically, a mind follows a common pattern of thinking. As a consequence of the common way or the mental model, mental distress can occur to a greater extent. This can be explained as follows. Mind tends to divide things into good and bad, with an underlying tendency to think only good should happen and can get too distracted easily if bad happens.

Mind that tends to think only bad things happen can get too much distress and anxiety every time such a thought comes up. This brings us to the question of how to let go of distress in distressing situations. First, to let go of distress, you may apply wisdom to understand that distress is a part of life. In doing so, try to take action to resolve matters causing distress and find peace in that. You may ensure you've done your part. Second, try to make the most of each moment, considering moments of peace as precious. Avoid giving too much value to your thoughts that hurt you, as what you don't value can't stay there too long, bothering you. It's a technique you can adopt to let go of self-view with wisdom.

An ordinary mind tends to divide things into likes and dislikes. In doing so, your mind is functioning in an ordinary mode, making you crave what you like and not want what you dislike. When such thoughts occur, simply understand that sometimes things can take on any face value; likes and dislikes can come into your experience. Then, understand, as long as you try your best to resolve things, that's all you can do with wisdom and to make the most of each moment, wise things, a way to renounce, developing the training that is noble, or letting go of delusion for self-view.

When you try to develop the noble path, most things you have to understand are related to the mind and its way of thinking. A mind tends to construct things even in the absence of real things. The mind tends to retain and surface data: past events and experiences, happy and hurtful things, and things that happened to you. It's not necessarily the data or information that comes to the surface of your mind that hurts you, but the way you understand them, and when you give too much value to such thoughts, they can make you suffer even if such events are gone, never to come back. In the same way, the mind can walk into the future, construct it, and live in it. The present moment of reality is gone before even the mind realizes it. In this way, what appears to be reality itself traps one in a delusion; it's more like a dream each person experiences, and if at some point someone happens to get stuck in the dream-like state with delusion, that tends to produce suffering.

The mind can construct various things even in the absence of such things. If someone happens to take all that the mind presents as valuable, true, and important without applying wisdom to understand beyond what the mind presents, one happens to get swept away in the waves of thoughts. When someone gets swept away in the wave of thoughts and senses that respond constantly to experiences, ups and downs of life, it tends to make them suffer.

Mind catches signals and presents a sense of self and worldly experiences for you, like a radio signal picking up what you tune in to, but what you tune in to is only one mode, or the common model grounded in delusion. In this way, the nature of the mind is that it tends to construct self and world based on delusion, and when you don't surpass what the mind presents to you as self and world with wisdom, suffering comes to be. When you surpass the common mode and understand self and world with noble wisdom by letting go of delusion, suffering ceases to be. To understand more about how energy can transform within, after cessation, you can surpass your current mode of mind-body with wisdom to understand the kinds of mind-bodies experienced in samsara or triple knowledge and beyond.

Every person has a shell around them that makes them unique. As individuals, people are diverse. Every human being has something inherently unique to them, so they think, experience, and react differently. Even when every person is a part of the universe, within the universe, each experience the world differently. No two people are the same in terms of how they understand and experience the world in their mental continuum. Yet, what is common to all is that and what you would typically experience is that when you immerse yourself in worldly experiences too much, you tend to experience inner fires within. The outside world is experienced within. The world and others are experienced within. Those who purify delusion within gets to understand those who have given up delusion within themselves.

Sometimes, a typical mind functions in a mode that can get stuck with the expectation that another person you trust should always be there for you. A mind can get stuck in the expectations that the people you would like to love and care for should love and care for you as you would like and expect of them. When your trustworthiness fails, and the person you expect to receive love and care doesn't meet your expectations, the mind tends to suffer, get hurt, or get angry, and so on. Yet, typically nobody can meet another person's expectations 100 percent for various reasons. By understanding this commonality and applying wisdom, you may reduce delusion toward the expectations you carry within. Instead, if you could fulfill your responsibilities towards all and find peace in that, you are more likely to experience sustainable peace of mind.

The mind functioning in the common mode generates fuel or ignites fires within. That fuel cyclically produces ongoing suffering. Every time you think of something delusional or engage in an intentional action, that generates fuel within. For example, when someone you dislike puts you down, and you catch the experience in your thoughts based on delusion again and again, instead of experiencing peace, you experience ongoing fires.

The universal law is that your intentional action generates fuel within you; each person generates their own fuel, and such fuel can make you suffer if it is unwholesome. What is unwholesome and what causes inner fires are grounded on delusion. Let go of the firing process can be done by letting go of delusion. You may carefully let go of delusion progressively; for example, if you've taken five precepts or monastic rules, you may now upgrade to the noble eight precepts. If you had lived a ritualistic life as a monk or a householder, you may now upgrade to go beyond rituals and experience Sotapanna. If you meditate in certain postures, stopping all usual activities, you may now maintain right understanding beyond convention during all activities during waking hours (i.e., develop noble concentration). If you have only known and attend to conventional Dhamma and Sangha in your mental continuum and in your intentional actions, you may now attend to universal Dhamma and Sangha. If you have read ancient books to understand nibbana or Sotapanna, as they cover only a very small percentage of matters related to universal Dhamma, you may now expand your knowledge to understand these matters better.

If you cry at losses or get too much upset, you may now stop crying or not get too much distress at losses by reflecting on universal Dhamma, taking it as an opportunity to develop wisdom, and cultivate a balanced mind state. If you had known only happiness coming from depending on worldly experience, now you may expand happiness beyond measurable or dependent things. If you are previously focused on breath or on your thoughts in a non-judgmental manner, you may now focus on your thoughts with wisdom. If you had only known Buddha's Dhamma at a societal level, you may now let go of a limited understanding to understand Buddha's Dhamma on the cosmic level. If you've previously heard Dhamma and Sangha matters in people and places where a high degree of rituals were followed, and none declared the practice through experience or the direct path to address the root cause of suffering, understand now you have an opportunity to hear how to let go of delusion, the root cause of suffering.

All communities of Sangha belong together, as their teachings are rooted in the universal Buddha. The only thing is, except for a very few, almost everyone in the Sangha community is an ordinary person; they teach you the basics. Whoever experiences Arahantship teaches you how to end the basic state and progress across the lower and upper stages of nibbana.

Different knowledge or understanding is not a reason to declare that one is inferior, superior, or the same as others; rather, all people are precious, a community of Sangha belonging together. The only thing people were unaware of for a thousand years, since the Buddha's parinirvana, was that no one explained all these things to you.

Just as undesirable plants reduce overall crop yield[3], ordinary views have reduced the percentage of Dhamma related to Sotapanna available to you within Sangha communities over a thousand years since Buddha parinirvana. There is a higher percentage of discussions about things not directly related to experiencing nibbana or Sotapanna, and an extremely low percentage of discussions about the four stages of nibbana. The outcome is that a rare noble view is held within the community. Typically, people who are bound to end samsara appear when there is an appearance of nibbana in human societies. They have the opportunity to hear about direct practices leading to nibbana, and when they do, they want to test them within themselves. As they develop Dhamma within, they are bound to be free from sufferings arising from delusions about the self and worldly experiences.

> "It is impossible, it cannot happen for an individual who experiences Sotapanna and beyond to cause various divisions within the Sangha based on conventions or a schism in the Saṅgha. But it is possible for an ordinary person to cause various divisions, a schism in the Saṅgha."- AN 1.275

---

[3] When Buddhas appear, they remove undesirable plants, revealing a field of high-quality crop yields meaning explaining things that are directly related to Sotapanna, revealing the noble view and the noble path applicable to all.

Dhamma and Sangha that divide are the conventional Dhamma and Sangha. Dhamma and Sangha that unite all is the universal Dhamma and Sangha. Buddha's Dhamma is the universal Dhamma. You can link conventional Dhamma and conventional Sangha to the universal Dhamma and universal Sangha, and to grow your understanding of what you already know to experience Sotapanna.

Chapter 6
Life experience and the noble path

Since birth, an average person knows only worldly happiness and pleasures but not the blissful experience of Sotapanna. Although life offers ample opportunities to train on the noble path in daily life, few ordinary people know how to awaken to wisdom and let go of their entanglement in the thought process and samsara.

Most people follow what is known, but few discover the unknown. Universal truths open only when you are willing to discover something new you have not experienced. Those unwilling to test practices or to seek questions and answers through wisdom fall off the path long before they experience Sotapanna. By understanding where you may be falling out of practice, you can improve. The mind that is trained to grasp self, rituals, and social practices over many years may initially struggle to give up deluded understanding about such things. Thus, a person's mind and its tendency to follow common ways can hinder their ability to complete the noble path to attain Sotapanna. This happens all too often, to the extent that many find it easier to resort to rituals, yet remain there, unable to grow beyond. Thus, it's important we talk about it, as Dhamma is to give up, taken as a raft, once you have something, whether it's rituals or lifestyles, or whatsoever it should merely be for the purpose of growth. Growth means letting go of delusion using the very same things that you have taken in before to support your practice, as it allows transforming to the lower stages of nibbana. Each time you practice something, you give up that practice to climb the next step, as you climb the ladder of four stages in the noble path. The noble path has four stages. When a person does not use the basics, rituals, or lifestyle to overcome delusion, they get stuck in delusion for many years or are unable to experience Sotapanna in their lifetime. Now that you hear these words, you may learn how to merely use whatever you practice for its purpose, and that is to let go of delusion. You may apply wisdom to let go of grasping self-view and social practices in your mind in your usual daily life. As you train the mind in daily life, remember that you will need to practice letting go when you face difficult circumstances. Initially, as you train to let go, you will struggle, but as you continue to do it over and over again, you will find it easier to let go. What typically happens is that it's not that one is walking to the noble path happily, but a person who is in distress and is seeking happiness, having not found happiness, or another way to experience peace and happiness in worldly life, gives up delusions by understanding life experience with wisdom while taking initial refuge in the universal Triple Gem. It's more like the life experience and the nature inviting you to understand the universal truths.

One reason an ordinary mind struggles to give up in difficult circumstances is that it can take someone to recognize the benefit of giving up. Staying with what's known or ordinary mind state may seem easier on the surface, but it brings suffering beneath the surface. An ordinary person has very little capacity. One can imagine very little about the bliss that awaits on the noble path, but vast remains unknown; the best experiences are yet to be discovered. As a matter of fact, people who suffer have two choices: either walk the noble path or suffer. Because universal truths do not disappear, people are naturally drawn toward nibbana. But walking the path is possible only for those with wisdom that allows them to understand beyond self and social practices. Once a person becomes a Sotapanna, they realize that nothing is more blissful[4] than experiencing the Sotapanna.

> "Which three? The appearance of the Tathāgatha, worthy & rightly self-awakened, is rare in the world. An Arahant who teaches the four stages of nibbana that goes beyond fetters (self-view, rituals, etc.) proclaimed by the Tathāgata is rare in the world. A person who is grateful & thankful is rare in the world."- Dullabha Sutta, AN 3.114

Being grateful to those who support, and aid is a sign of being a good person. To experience Sotapanna, you may

---

[4] Once a person becomes a Sotapanna, they realize that their former life as an ordinary person cannot compare to the life they experience in mind as a Sotapanna.

cultivate good qualities and integrity. Even an average, good person would always be thankful to those who have helped. A noble person indicates you have a higher degree of what it takes to be a good person and beyond. For example, a grateful child would always be thankful to good parents and teachers alike.

> "But anyone who rouses his unbelieving mother & father, settles & establishes them in noble understanding of dhamma; rouses his unvirtuous mother & father, settles & establishes them in noble virtue… to this extent one pays & repays one's mother & father."- Kataññu Suttas, AN 2.31-32

The best a person can repay their gratitude to those who have helped them and are seeking stable peace or nibbana is to support them in experiencing nibbana because it cuts off suffering with stability. The best support you can provide to those who seek nibbana; whether it's your former teachers, or current teachers, those with whom you associate, or strangers, is to allow them to develop the noble view[5], which enables them

---

[5] "Arahant Sariputta, in his former ordinary life, was born to brahmin parents in Upatissa village; hence, he was named Upatissa. His mother was Sari. His very close friend was Kolita, another brahmin youth, son of Moggali. Both youths were searching for the right doctrine that would lead them to liberation from the round of rebirths, and both were seeking the universal truths and a teacher. First, they went to Sancaya, but they were not satisfied because they could not experience true freedom from his teaching. Then they wandered all over Jambudipa looking for a teacher who would show them the way to freedom or Deathless nibbana, but their search was fruitless. After some time, they went their separate ways, but with the understanding that the one who found the true version of dhamma or nibbana first should inform the other."- Dhp 392

to enter the universally applicable path. You may treat all with immense respect and care. Treating all with immense respect and care is a sign of boundless loving kindness, whereas dividing people and providing different treatment to people categorically is a sign of an ordinary mind state. You may grow beyond ordinary loving kindness to develop boundless loving kindness based on the noble view. A noble person would be immensely grateful to the universal Buddha for providing the incomparable bliss; Sotapanna, and beyond. Having completed the training and experienced cessation, those who bear the final body have one task: to share nibbana or Sotapanna with those who seek it to end their suffering. Hearing the noble path for an ordinary person becomes possible only when the sharer has completed the four stages of nibbana. Thus, spiritual friends who aspire to represent the Buddha may initially develop Sotapanna within and share with others.

> "One should act as one teaches others; only with oneself thoroughly tamed should one tame other. To tame oneself is, indeed, difficult." - Dhp 159

Chapter 7
Why hearing Sotapanna is rare?

Getting an opportunity to hear the universally applicable nibbana is rare. And when they hear those who feel like testing it, it's rare, and as a consequence, noble disciples are rare. This can be explained as follows. Many practitioners claim to follow the Buddha's Dhamma, but those willing to investigate Dhamma matters with wisdom are more likely to understand the universally applicable noble path. If you were to investigate Dhamma with wisdom, you should be able to comprehend that what Buddha has said is not something an ordinary person knows. What common people know is what social constructs are, and what Buddha has said is something that's happening at the universal level, universal laws, something beyond common ways of understanding self and worldly experiences or conventions. What is not visible to social practices and to sensory information alone is what lies beyond common things: the universal rhythm, universal laws, and nibbana; a happening at the universal level, experienced in a person's mental continuum.

Society is known to ordinary people. The universe is known to Buddhas. Ordinary people can develop an understanding beyond a limited, conventional understanding of self and the universe, across the stages of nibbana, and by developing the triple knowledge while living, which is a perfect quality of the perfect universal Dhamma.

What is common is that most people, and almost everyone, know how to be happy temporarily by associating with those they like, doing things they like, engaging in various things and practices, including meditation, jhanas, and the like. Almost everyone knows how to eat well, dress well, live well in society, make a living, and so on. What is unknown to most people is how to find stable happiness and peace of mind without having to make any significant changes to what they eat, dress, or do to make a living, and how they live in the community within usual activities by cutting off the root of suffering: delusion, in the mental continuum. That's what the universally applicable noble path reveals to you.

Certain principles and techniques applicable to discovering things through modern scientific methods also apply to the testing of universal Dhamma. Formulating a research question, or the question one is going to find an answer based on evidence, is a basic thing scientist do before conducting research or discovery. After formulating a research question, the thing that they are going to address, the next step is to specify the assumptions that are going to be tested (or "hypothesis testing' known in scientific language). Accepting or refusing something without testing for its validity leads to false beliefs. Getting rid of false beliefs is a way to discover the truth. The same can be applied to testing the universal truth or Buddha's universal Dhamma. This can be explained further as follows.

If someone recommends practices but has not experienced nibbana through them, their recommendations are not valid, even for themselves. Then, to know more about reliable practices to experience nibbana, there is a need to know who experiences such states in the community. When someone shares Dhamma without declaring their understanding of Dhamma through personal experience, the validity of what they say is missing, and thus, there is nothing to test. On the other hand, when someone declaring their understanding of Dhamma through personal experience, it becomes possible to assume something as valuable or sufficiently valid reason for wanting to test the practices. To keep the mode of discovery alive and to open up possibilities for testing, the universal Buddha adopted self-declaration of the understanding of nibbana himself and approved and endorsed keeping the golden noble standards of self-declaring Dhamma knowledge after experiencing it for oneself with the community. Thus, self-declaration of knowledge is the noble standard and golden standard in the noble path that has been tested, approved, and recommended by the Buddhas and what has been followed through by his universal disciples. Typically, those who truly experience Arahantship tend to openly declare their experience. This brings us to discuss the point that over a thousand years, there has been an ongoing discussion about Buddha's Dhamma. After Buddha's Parinirvana, people living in monasteries and homes have changed Dhamma; added many things, omitted many things, and interpreted what the Buddha said differently over time. As a result, today, many people talk about Buddha's Dhamma, but they propose various practices; thus, a truth seeker will have to adopt a mode of discovery and answer some key questions.

Q.1: Different people suggest different practices, suggesting that you practice them to experience nibbana. Thus, among many ways and many things' people say and ways of explaining Buddha's Dhamma, how do you discover the true version of Dhamma that is universally applicable to all or universal truth among many versions?

A.1: Whoever describes Dhamma as explained by the Buddha; universal happening based on universal laws of karma, and wisdom, and the universal training path is about can cutting off the root cause of suffering regardless of surface; let go of delusion (i.e. unwholesome) or restricted understanding of conventional self, social practices, and doubts, represents Buddha's Dhamma.

Q.2: In line with noble standards, to know who experiences such states, each person may self-declare by taking the responsibility for what they share or say regarding the Buddha's universal Dhamma. Not taking responsibility and hiding away are non-noble; thus, when someone declares practices with confidence but without stating whether they helped them achieve nibbana, that is a non-noble or ordinary way. Also, when someone declares Dhamma matters and falsely claims they have experienced Sotapanna or nibbana through such practices, that is a non-noble way. Thus, a person whose seek truth has a question to address: how do you recognize true Dhamma among many versions of Dhamma and true Sangha within the community?

A.2: Whoever described Dhamma as described by the Buddha and within whom such Dhamma practices are perfectly established; so they are not grasping social practices themselves, not having greed for self (i.e don't expect to make a living out of Dhamma or expect gains or honour), they have let go of delusion for conventional understanding of self, they have no doubts, they are not proud, they don’t have ill will, and gone beyond dependant happiness and ten fetters, in other words what they say and explain as universal Dhamma is what is perfectly established within them, that is a representation of universal Sangha.

> "Even so, Vaccha, that material shape by which one recognising the Tathāgata (or his universal disciples) might recognise him, that material shape has been got rid of by the Tathāgata (or his universal disciples), cut off at the root, made like a palm-tree stump that can come to no further existence and is not liable to arise again in the future. Freed from denotation by material shape is the Tathāgata (or his universal disciples), Vaccha, he is deep, immeasurable, unfathomable as is the great ocean. 'Arises' does not apply, 'does not arise' does not apply, 'both arises and does not arise' does not apply, 'neither arises nor does not arise' does not apply."- Aggivacchasutta, MN 72

> "And how is a person of no integrity endowed with qualities of no integrity? There is the case where a person of no integrity is lacking in noble understanding, lacking in their ability to do the right thing, lacking in concern for the results of unskillful actions; one is not understanding Sotapanna, lazy, of muddled mindfulness, & poor discernment. This is how a person of lack of integrity is endowed with qualities of lack of integrity."- Cula-punnama Sutta, MN 110

One of the barriers faced by a wise ordinary person when attempting to practice the universal Dhamma or let go of delusion is that they may understand how to let go of delusion as it is explained to them. Still, they may constantly struggle to let go of delusion through daily life experiences and to renounce grasping the fetters with stability in their mental continuum. This explains why, in general, the four stages of nibbana take time to develop, subject to each person's wisdom and karma, regardless of surface factors. Thus, when the resources are available, such as the universally applicable training path to let go of delusion for self, social practices, doubt is revealed to you, you may hear it and apply again and again, and let go of delusion. If you would like to test this practice as a consequence, what you will experience is less suffering. Every time you renounce the world with wisdom, you will experience happiness and peace at that moment, and gradually build the practice and stabilise it through both conscious effort and nature's way.

> "I don't praise wrong practice for all practitioners, regardless of whether they live in a monastery or at home. Because of improper practice, all practitioners, regardless of whether they live in a monastery or at home, do not succeed in the system of skillful teaching.
>
> And what's the wrong practice? It is a non-noble or wrong view, a wrong thought...
>
> I praise noble practice for all practitioners, regardless of whether they live in a monastery or at home. Because of noble practice, all practitioners, regardless of whether they live in a monastery or at home, succeed in the system of skillful teaching. And what's the right practice? It is the noble right view..."- Dutiyapaṭipadāsutta, SN 45.24
>
> "Furthermore, a noble disciple has experiential confidence in the universal teaching: 'The universal Dhamma is well explained by the Buddha—apparent in the present life, immediately effective, inviting

> inspection, relevant, so that wise people can know it for themselves.' This is the second kind of overflowing merit and wholesome ..."- Dutiyapuññābhisandasutta, AN 4.52

You may make use of universal Buddha, universal Dhamma, and universal Sanga to develop wholesome thoughts in nature's way, while bearing in mind that you only need to hear noble Dhamma until you find noble Dhamma within you. You only need to associate with the noble Sangha until you become the noble Sangha within you at the last stage of nibbana. You become free from sila and monastic rules when you let go of delusion regarding the first three fetters, and when you find the Triple Gem within you across the stages of nibbana. Thus, you need to carefully follow each step to train in certain ways and to find freedom from what helped you train, fully independent and free across the stages of the nibbana.

Chapter 8
Testing Dhamma

To experience stable peace (or Sotapanna) within daily life, a practitioner requires testing their faith. What exactly is the faith you require testing?

If you have faith that the self and your worldly experiences are empty of a permanent self, and that losses and gains, ups and downs, are part of life, that is your faith.

You may begin your Dhamma practice by testing your faith in the universal Dhamma within daily life. To do that, when you experience difficult circumstances, apply Dhamma wholeheartedly to experience the world with wisdom, so you don't hurt yourself or others; resolve things that can be resolved (wholesome) without too much worrying or getting anxious about such experiences and alike (unwholesome). In other words, when you have worrying thoughts, understand that worrying situations are part of life, and thus, as much as possible, keep worries and alike down by applying wisdom through conscious efforts while attending to tasks that need doing within your usual life. Similarly, when you have thoughts of anger surfacing in your mind, whether it's towards your circumstances, or with those you associate with, such as family members, friends or a stranger, or when others blame you or put you down, do not harbour ill will or the intention to cause them harm, even in a random thought, as such thoughts generate fires within; instead, find peace and happiness in not harboring ill will. Furthermore, let go of delusions regarding excessive likes, dislikes, and expectations you have for worldly experiences in mind, give up pretending, give up the need to compare one another as people, give up conceit, avoid sharing wrong views of Dhamma while making the best of life at each moment.

How to make the best of life? Not becoming sad over sad experiences or not dwelling on them; instead, take action to resolve things, fulfill obligations, and find happiness and peace in that, is a way to make the best of worldly experience. In this manner, giving priority to happiness and peace in a way that is not harming oneself or another is the noble Dhamma living; so, you may choose to eat the best, wear the best, associate with the best, learn the best, do activities you have to do the best, enjoy what you like doing while letting go of delusion for such things with wisdom and live life at each moment the best initially, by enhancing happiness and peace in Dhamma ways (or wholesome manner not hurting oneself or another).

To grow in noble wisdom, you may train the mind to let go of delusions based on worldly experience during difficult times; as often happens during easy times, there is nothing to give up, or things that bring you pain, by cutting the root of the delusion. Then, as you train to cut off delusion during difficult times, there will again be a time when things go easy. Then, try to understand that what is easy can change as well; thus, enjoy what you like without developing delusion. If you continue to train your mind this way, you will begin to stabilise your mind and experience freedom and immeasurable, beyond-dependent happiness, or happiness that depends on worldly experiences, with wisdom.

Importantly, understand that the only way to understand the universal Buddha and universal Sangha is to understand universal Dhamma within. When you understand yourself beyond conventions with wisdom, you get to understand the universal Triple Gem within. You may remind yourself that nibbana is not something you see from outside, or something you see merely through sensory information, but something you understand beyond sensory information with wisdom within you.

> “Friends, even if a person, grabbing hold of my robe, following right behind me and placing his feet in my footsteps, were having thoughts of likes or greediness for worldly experiences based on delusion, strongly attached to worldly experiences, if they have ill will, they don't give-up grasping self-view and social practices with wisdom, thus they cannot retain noble view in their mental continuum but are lacking noble mindfulness, lacking noble understanding, noble

> concertation, confused and ignoble, and living with uncontrolled desires for worldly experiences based on delusion, then he would be far from me, as I am from him.
>
> What is the reason? Because, friends, that person (or monk) does not develop universal Dhamma within or understand or see the Dhamma within. Not seeing the Dhamma, he does not see me. But friends, if there is a person who develop noble wisdom and noble qualities within lives a far away he would be very close to me, and I would be very close to him. why? Because, friends, that person does develop universal Dhamma within, understand or see the Dhamma within. Seeing the universal Dhamma, he see me."- Sanghāṭikaṇṇa Sutta, Itv 92
>
> "One who finds joy and happiness in the universal Dhamma teaching succeeds, but a person who dislikes the universal Dhamma meets their downfall."- Parābhavasutta, snp 1.6

It's helpful to understand potential obstacles to developing the noble path. One obstacle is that if you were to wait to see universal Buddha, universal Dhamma, and universal Sangha from the outside, merely through sensory information, chances are they will not get to see the Triple Gem. This is because what is visible to sensory information is conventions and social practices; what is not directly visible to sensory information is the Triple Gem.

Supreme Buddhahood is an experience for the supreme Buddha. For great Arahants of the past, such as Arahant

Sariputta, the supreme Buddha was a supreme Buddha without a doubt through personal experience. For an unwise conventional bhikkhu at the time, such as Devadatta, the supreme Buddha was not a supreme Buddha, and had doubts about the supreme Buddha. The same can be applicable today. For people who experience Arahantship today, the supreme Buddha is, without a doubt, the supreme Buddha through personal experience. Ordinary people hear that the supreme Buddha is a supreme Buddha, but don't have experimental confidence in the supreme Buddha unless they experience at least the Sotapanna mind state within. In this manner, it's not that the supreme Buddha lacks supreme Buddhahood qualities, but if someone lacks similar wisdom or qualities within, they don't get to experience Buddhahood within, and they don't get to understand Buddhahood in another, as each person makes sense, interprets, and understands another person within themselves. Thus, as one purifies oneself from the delusional understanding of the universal Dhamma by letting go of delusion for the fetters including self-view, they can experience renunciation; a stable peace of mind, and the universal Buddha and the universal Sangha who experience nibbana across stages within.

"Shraddha,"or "Sadda"; the meaning emerging from universal Dhamma makes sense to you, and if you happen to maintain confirmed confidence in what you hear, that is what helps you to experience nibbana, or Sotapanna. If you happen to understand your life experience with wisdom by hearing and understanding the meaning of universally applicable Dhamma words that go beyond mental fetters, including self-view, social practices to begin with, that is how you develop experimental confidence or confirmed confidence in Dhamma. Faith in universal Dhamma, which develops into experimental confidence, joy, and rupture, is essential for making progress in the noble eightfold path across stages.

> "When a noble disciple recollects the Realized One their mind is not full of greed, hate, and delusion. At that time their mind is quite unswerving, based on the Realized One. A noble disciple whose mind is unswerving finds inspiration in the meaning and the teaching, and finds joy connected with the teaching. When they're joyful, rapture springs up. When the mind is full of rapture, the body becomes tranquil. "-Mahānāmasutta, AN 6.10

Nibbana is a progressive process. The lower stages differ from the upper stages. One has to carefully let go of one's deluded understanding of self with wisdom across the stages of nibbana. Nibbana is something that is out there in the universe at all times; you need to make an interlink to connect with it while you are living by adopting the practice in your mental continuum.

Chapter 9
Giving up

Give up everything at once, if you want to experience Sotapanna. If you give up materials and shape external things but retain deluded understanding regarding your thoughts, mental frameworks, schemas, and mental construction, you will continue to experience mental distress or sufferings coming from worldly experiences. If you retain materials, whether you shape or not shape external things, but give up deluding understanding of your thoughts, mental frameworks, and mental construction, you will continue to let go of experiencing mental distress or sufferings coming from worldly experiences. When someone experiences Sotapanna (Sakadagami etc.), their external appearance or surroundings do not necessarily change, but their state of mind does, so that a person who used to be sad becomes happy with stability (i.e., a kind of happiness unknown to ordinary people) and never to be sad again. A person who used to engage in unwholesome intentional actions will not do the same again.

> “Ever since I was born in the noble birth, sister, I don’t recall having intentionally taken the life of a living creature. By this truth, may both you and your baby be safe.”- Aṅgulimālasutta, MN 86

Then, out of compassion for the community of friends, those who experience Arahantship will declare their understanding of the four stages of nibbana or nibbana. However, if you focus on external factors and social practices, instead of focusing on their understanding of universal Dhamma (i.e. noble right view), you will miss the opportunity to meet the universal Dhamma and the noble Sangha. Instead, if you develop the ability to understand the in-depth meaning of higher Dhamma that is shared regardless of whoever shares, you will meet universal Dhamma or Sotapanna within as you progress in Dhamma and Vinaya or discipline.

When it comes to nibbana, there is one progressive Dhamma practice and fruition, and Vinaya practice and fruition for all: Sotapanna, Sakadagami, Anagami, and Arahant. The reason is that rules (precepts or monastic rules) are helpful and needed to control underlying desires for self and excessive sensual pleasures of an ordinary mind, regardless of whether one lives in a monastery or at home. Freedom from rules across the stages of nibbana cuts off delusion for sensual pleasures and ill for an Anagami. Thus, the path to Sotapanna, or developing Dhamma and Vinaya, doesn't require maintaining celibacy through personal compulsion, although those who prefer celibacy through rules may continue to choose to let go of delusion, as each person has to understand freedom within their experiences and choices, not outside. If you've had enough of worldly sufferings and are seeking to let go of mental distress with stability, you may continue on your choices but understand beyond your choices with wisdom to let go of delusion regarding self-view and conventions, and doubts to experience Sotapanna. As a Sotapanna progresses, they cut off the root of sensual desires; deluded understanding that worldly experiences are pleasurable and that pleasures are stable when they experience the Anagami state in mind, regardless of external factors, including the presence or absence of people.

Limits such as self-view and social practices bind you to the worldly experiences, and limited knowledge makes you suffer. “Sadda” the meaning emerging from these words that goes beyond the conventional understanding of self makes sense to you, and if you happen to maintain confirmed confidence in what you hear, that is what helps you to experience Sotapanna or nibbana. Conditional faith, meaning your faith that depends on external factors, social practices and alike, that’s dependent faith. Instead, if you happen to understand your life experience with wisdom by hearing and understanding the meaning of Dhamma words that go beyond mental fetters, including self-view, social practices to begin with, that is how you develop experimental confidence or confirmed confidence in Dhamma. If nibbana were to depend on convention, when convention changes, nibbana should change. If nibbana were in an appearance, dress, buildings, and the like, when such things change, nibbana should change. If nibbana were consciousness, when consciousness changes, nibbana should change. Conscious efforts alone cannot help you experience Sotapanna because consciousness is subject to change. This explains why the training path to Sotapanna includes both conscious efforts and nature's support to develop and maintain the noble right view regarding the fetters and in the middle way. Nature's support is that when you expand your mental energy by linking with those free from mental fetters, your mental energy grows and aligns with what they experience in line with universal laws and functioning. If you were to attempt to see energy transformation through sensory information alone, as they are limited, such as eyes, it will usually not be possible to see because eyes are designed to detect a very narrow band of visible light; it's as if they are tuned into a specific "station". Similarly, the understanding of an ordinary mind state is limited as it's restricted to the common mode, a particular mode. Yet if you were to surpass sensory information with wisdom, self-view, and other fetters, you will understand it within you as you develop higher stages of nibbana, triple knowledge and beyond. In any case, a person can understand everything within, not outside, and the path to Sotapanna reveals how to develop such an understanding.

> "When five fearful animosities have subsided in a noble disciple, and one possesses the four factors of

stream-entry, one could by oneself declare of oneself: 'I am one finished with hell, finished with the animal realm, finished with the domain of ghosts, finished with the plane of misery, the bad destinations, the nether world. I am a stream-enterer, no longer bound to the nether world, fixed in destiny, with final stage of enlightenment as my destination.'

What are the four factors of stream-entry that one possesses? Here, friends, the noble disciple possesses confirmed confidence in the Buddha thus: 'The Blessed One is an arahant, perfectly enlightened, accomplished in true knowledge and conduct, fortunate, knower of the world, unsurpassed leader of persons to be tamed, teacher of devas and humans, the Enlightened One, the Blessed One.'

He possesses confirmed confidence in the universal Dhamma thus: 'The universal Dhamma is well expounded by the Blessed One, directly visible, immediate, inviting one to come and see, applicable, to be personally experienced by the wise.'

He possesses confirmed confidence in the universal Saṅgha thus: 'The trainee Saṅgha of the Blessed One's disciples is practising the good way, practising the straight way, practising the true way, practising the proper way; and Arahants have finished their practice, thus, the four pairs of persons (Sotapanna, etc.), the eight types of individuals—this universal or noble Saṅgha of the Blessed One's disciples is worthy of gifts, worthy of hospitality, worthy of offerings, worthy of reverential salutation, the unsurpassed field of merit for the world.'

He possesses the noble virtues, freedom from precepts and monastic rules—unbroken, untorn,

> unblemished, unmottled, freeing, praised by the wise, ungrasped, leading to noble concentration.
>
> These are the four factors of stream-entry that one possesses."- Pañcaverabhayasutta, SN 12.41
>
> "By hearing the words of higher Dhamma, Uggasena, who was still on top of the pole, attained Arahatship."- Dhp 348
>
> "By hearing the words of higher Dhamma both the bride and bridegroom attained Sotapatti Fruition."- Dhp 202

Practice to maintain and experience peace of mind (or the noble path) can be developed by hearing, understanding and applying certain techniques and training. People do things they later regret, and sometimes they regret doing certain things. Yet if someone repeatedly does things they regret, they constantly engage in things that steal away their peace. Thus, one technique you can develop to train the noble path or piece of mind is to not think, say, or do things you regret later on. For example, Angulimala killed many people due to a misunderstanding, but he learned from his mistake and stopped doing such things again; thus, to find peace of mind, a person needs to learn from mistakes and not do things they later regret again and again.

Some people hide their weaknesses, delusions about themselves and the world, greed, and hate by pretending to be great to themselves. In this manner, if you hide yourself from yourself, you can't develop the noble path. Another technique you can use to train in the noble path or peace of mind is to not hide your weaknesses (or delusions about worldly experiences, greed, and hate) from yourself at first. For example, sometimes an untrained mind will encourage you not to look at your mistakes or weaknesses, but to look for others' mistakes and weaknesses without necessarily looking into yourself, taking up the time you would otherwise spend investigating yourself. The reason why some people hide their delusion for themselves, act as if they are better than others (as people) and alike is wanting to preserve and protect their "self-view", and as a consequence they are likely to experience fires within. The lack of wisdom and getting caught by your hidden mind can make you suffer. Instead, you may reveal your mind to yourself and develop wisdom to reduce stress. In another example, some people act and speak as if they know all about nibbana or sotapanna, even when they can't explain things that are directly relevant to four stages of nibbana, is that they want to protect their "ego, or self-view" and pretend to know it all in the absence of true knowledge for gains and honours, or merely to feel good about themselves. One has to make an attempt at something only because one does not have it as yet; yet, as a Sotapanna has found peace beyond self and social practices, no attempt is needed to feel good about anything.

Typically, someone associates with another person wanting something in exchange, including a feeling of altruism or satisfaction, or the perception that someone or something belongs to oneself and alike. Whenever someone or something belongs to oneself, or when one associates with someone expecting something, and when changes happen in self, others, and the world, such things can produce suffering in the mind of those who touch them again and again. The association or idea of belonging as seen from outside is not necessarily the root cause of suffering, but delusion (and greed and hate, or likes and dislikes, two sides of mental attachment based on the deluded understanding of self and worldly experience). This explains why Sotapanna is a mind state; you may develop wisdom regardless of external factors. Typically, only noble friends associate with others without any expectation. Some spiritual friends misinterpret saying Dhamma is in words, yet Dhamma is not in words, but in the way one understands words to get as close as possible to an understanding of at least a Sotapanna. The meaning emerging from the words of universal Dhamma lies beyond self-view, rituals, and social practices and can only be understood by certain ordinary wise people who have the instinct to discern its deeper meaning beyond mere words. Thus, a Sotapanna (Sakadagami, etc.) is rare.

> "Now in this regard, Cunda, you should work on self-effacement in each of the following ways.

> Others will have ordinary, common or wrong view, but here we will have the noble view (right view).
>
> Others will have ordinary, common or wrong thought, but here we will have right thought…"- Sallekhasutta, MN 8
>
> "A person who is an inquirer of universal truth, unable to encompass another person's mind, should investigate an Arahant regarding Dhamma related matters; the Realized One for two things—things that can be seen and heard: 'Can anything corrupt meaning delusion regarding the fetters (self, social practices etc.) be seen or heard in the Realized One or not?' - Meaning, do they explain Dhamma as social practice, social truth, ritual, and the like, similar to the majority of ordinary people? Scrutinizing Arahants, they find that nothing corrupt can be seen or heard in the Realized Ones."- Vīmaṁsakasutta, MN 47

When you use wrong training and techniques, regardless of whether you remember what was in ancient books, follow the ritual, live a lifestyle in a monastery or at home, seek the universal truths, or nothing can help you experience peace of mind with stability or the universal happening, Sotapanna or nibbana. Those who want to train the mind to peace, you may constantly train your mind to let go of delusions regarding the fetters to renounce distress within usual activities.

Chapter 10
Understanding relationships

To understand universal truths, one may examine and understand deep truths about one's worldly experiences that are not easily visible or revealed to the surface with wisdom. For example, to a greater extent, what is commonly thought of as 'love' in societies is a state in which a person with a self-view looks after another person for some kind of benefit, pleasure or satisfaction for the self. Among the general population, there are ordinary good people who do things that are beneficial for others. To a greater extent they are driven by empathy, sympathy, self-satisfaction, altruism, compassion, and kindness, with an underlying tendency to think self and others are stable (i.e., delusion). Thus, even for an ordinary good person, changes in worldly experiences can cause distress.

In general, even in a parent-child relationship, parents and children expect certain things from one another. Expecting won't necessarily cause suffering. However, not understanding that all expectations[6] cannot be fulfilled can cause suffering. For example, a father may expect a son or daughter to get a well-paid job and support them financially. Yet, if the son or

[6] Not having the right view about the root cause of suffering can cause suffering.

daughter fails to get a job in a poor labour market, some parents may see it as a failure of a child's ability to look after them, or children may look at their parents as having failed to look after them for various reasons that are beyond the control of parents and so on. Daily life is where you have to practice Dhamma. Dhamma practice is mostly about giving up delusion. The purpose of Dhamma is not to ask one to stop doing things one likes, or to avoid gaining joys in the way one likes, but to reduce sufferings within things you like, dislikes and worldly experiences in a way that you don't hurt yourself or others. Thus, how can one understand relationships with wisdom (i.e. noble path) to enhance happiness and reduce stress?

Intentionally ignoring and not contributing to another's well-being is non-dhamma, but ignoring due to circumstances beyond one's control is not necessarily relevant to the purity of one's intention.

> "Intention, I tell you, is kamma. Intending, one does kamma by way of body, speech, & intellect."-Nibbedhikasutta, AN 6.63

Not hurting oneself or others by applying wisdom is Dhamma. This means with regard to relationships, to follow noble path, you may try your best to care for yourself and others and not to overly worry as it's unwise to worry if you are unable to care due to circumstances or reasons beyond one's control.

> "All those who want to train the noble path; path of noble ones of the past, future, and present, they may purify their intentions and intentional actions after repeatedly checking."- Ambalaṭṭhikarāhulovādasutta, MN 61

This brings us to discuss the famous contemporary view or the wrong view that an ordinary monk should teach or share the Dhamma with ordinary householders, and ordinary householders should provide materials for the benefit of the monk, a conditional relationship. Yet, if you were to question; what if a conventional monk or nun does not know about Sotapanna or nibbana? Then are they pressured into teaching any kind of views, even those that are not aligned with Sotapanna, while, firstly, lying to themselves and, secondly, lying to others? Being pressured into acting or pretending to know all about Buddha's perfect Dhamma is never appropriate; instead, one may create space for discovery, as this will help those who seek to escape suffering. Thus, out of boundless loving kindness and for the benefit of those in monasteries and homes, there is a need to reveal the universal noble path that allows one to escape suffering in a stable manner.

It is not easy to interpret every word of Dhamma in line with the four stages of nibbana and Sotapanna for someone who has not experienced it. When shared, wrong views have prevented noble views for centuries and are not beneficial for spiritual friends in any setting. This explains why, if someone divides Dhamma or Sangha by claiming they have different practices for experiencing universal Dhamma with an unwholesome intent, this can prevent them from having the opportunity to experience Sotapanna and beyond.

> "One day, the Buddha asked Devadatta if it was true that he was trying to create a schism in the community of Sangha Order, and he admitted that it was so. The Buddha warned him that it was a very serious offence."- Dhp 163

Spiritual friends may support one another to developing the right view, also in any other way including providing material support or any other support without limiting support to socially acceptable ways. That is because socially acceptable ways put limits, but noble way has no limits or boundless, one may support another in whatever the way one can. This is one way in which you can develop boundless loving kindness based on the right view, noble path.

What is commonly taught as Dhamma across societies has led you to understand yourself in terms of social frameworks and to be conditioned by conventional identities: a man, a woman, a young person, an old person, a monk, a householder, and so on. Those who want to understand emptiness, whatever understanding you have about yourself that is conditioned on social identities, social roles, rituals and social practices are impermanent, and must be understood as "not mine". Letting go of the restricted understanding you have of yourself, conditioned by social identities, social roles, and social practices with wisdom, leads to developing the right view, and boundless freedom and peace, and path to nibbana or Sotapanna.

When a true Sotapanna (Sakadagami etc.) says, "I am a Sotapanna," they mean that their mind (mental continuum) is free from a deluded understanding of self-based on social frameworks, rituals, conventions, and free from an underlying tendency to be conditioned by common identities. If one understands impermanence in nature with a lack of wisdom, it can lead to sadness, anxiety, frustrations and the like. If one understands the impermeable nature with wisdom, it can lead to reduced sadness, anxiety, frustrations and the like. What you see, hear, smell, and sense through your senses is the conventional understanding of worldly experience. What you don't see, hear, smell, and likewise merely through sensory information is nibbana. This explains why the noble path; the way to understand Sotapanna within is through noble wisdom, noble right view, and the understanding of the self beyond rituals, social practices, and conventions (i.e. noble path).

Chapter 11
Doing vs. Experiencing

When someone say "I am a monk", "I am a householder", "I am a meditation practitioner", and likewise, they are describing what they do or roles they play as these are conventional ways of describing things people do or roles they play. When someone say "I am a Sotapanna (or stream-enterer)", "I am an Anagami", "I am an Arahant"; these are conventional ways of describing what people experience in their thoughts, mental continuum. What people do (or the roles they play) are deeds or actions that generate karma again and again. What people experience in mind (Sotapanna, Anagami, etc) indicates intentions (or actions performed without grasping the fetters) or a state of freedom from karma across stages regardless of what they do.

> "Intention, I tell you, is kamma. Intending, one does kamma by way of body, speech, & intellect."- Nibbedhika Sutta, AN 6.63

Actions can be performed by the people who experience noble mind states without grasping the conventional understanding of self, social practices, and other fetters. This is the base of Buddha's Dhamma; nibbana across stages. When you do not develop universal Dhamma within, your mind can cheat you and guide you towards the wrong direction. Thinking of a representation of Buddha, you may get caught up in Mara merely because Mara can come in the appearance of a Buddha.

> "The Blessed One continued, "Friends, that non-human being had been an evil monk in the Kassapa Buddha's time. As a result of that bad kamma, he was boiled in hell for many years, for many hundreds of years, for many thousands of years, for many hundreds of thousands of years. As a remaining result of that same kamma, he has been reborn as a ghost and is experiencing such terrible pain."- Pāpabhikkhusutta, SN 19.17

Sotapanna does not divide people based on conventions, rituals, or social practices, but divides beings based only on ordinary and noble wisdom. What you see, hear, smell, and sense through your senses is the conventional understanding of worldly experience. What you don't see, hear, smell, and likewise merely through sensory information is nibbana. The only way to understand universal Dhamma within is through noble wisdom and noble right view; the understanding of the self beyond conventions, and other fetters (i.e. noble path). Ordinary wisdom can help you succeed in the material world. Noble wisdom can aid in success in both the material and spiritual world.

What is noble wisdom? Wisdom is to understand the self beyond the conventional understanding of self. Understand that every time you cling to your own understanding of self and worldly experiences based on standard social practices and conventions, with an underlying tendency to think they are stable, that is a weak mind, or a mind that is not trained enough to meet the noble path. Try to observe your thoughts, as they change and rise in line with social practices and understand the weakness of mind as it grasps self-view based on social practices. When you experience losses and when expectations fail, if you experience sadness or overly worry, understand that your mind functions in the common mode; the way that you have been told to think since childhood. Instead, to practice the noble path and develop wisdom, understand that losses and failed expectations are part of life, nothing too much to worry or get anxious about, as worries can make you hurt, not beneficial or wise. Do your best to resolve them without overly worrying, making the best of life experience at each moment as it occurs. The practice of noble path indicates that you maintain the wisdom-based right view, during waking hours, rather than meditating as a separate activity with an underlying tendency to maintain delusion regarding the self and conventions. You may try to maintain the wisdom-based right view during usual activities.

> "Any kind of feeling, all kind of perception, all consciousness should be seen as it really is with correct wisdom: 'This is not mine as there are no

> stable things coming from sensory information, this I am not, this is not myself.'
>
> Seeing in this way, the instructed noble disciple becomes disillusioned with form, disillusioned with feeling, disillusioned with perception, disillusioned with volitional formations, disillusioned with consciousness. Being disillusioned, one becomes dispassionate. Through dispassion one's mind is liberated. When it is liberated there comes the knowledge: 'It's liberated.' One understands: 'Rebirth has ended. The spiritual journey has been completed. What had to be done to end suffering has been done. There will be no rebirth."- Anattalakkhaṇa Sutta, SN 22.59

In general, most spiritual friends around the world have not met a true noble person or noble people for centuries; Sotapanna, Sakadagami, Anagami, Arahant. Thus, they have no idea what exactly the experience of mind states, Sotapanna and other states. Most spiritual friends don't know the mind state of Arahants but you may understand better now as the noble path is revealed to you. They are soft toward others and hard toward themselves, meaning they don't have expectations for themselves (based on delusion) but do have good thoughts toward others. People who experience noble mind states don't put any conscious effort into maintaining them; they are natural occurrences common to all Buddhas and Arahants.

> "Ānanda, those who you have sympathy for, and those worth listening to—friends and colleagues, relatives and family—should be encouraged,

> supported, and established in three things. What three?
>
> Experiential confidence in the Buddha: 'That Blessed One is perfected, a fully awakened Buddha, accomplished in knowledge and conduct, holy, knower of the world, supreme guide for those fit for training, teacher of gods and humans, awakened, blessed.'
>
> Experiential confidence in the universally applicable teaching: 'The teaching is well explained by the Buddha—apparent in the present life, immediately effective, inviting inspection, relevant, so that sensible people can know it for themselves.'
>
> Experiential confidence in the universal Saṅgha: 'The trainee noble Saṅgha of the Buddha's disciples is practicing the way that's good, direct, systematic, and proper. Arahants have completed the training. It consists of the four pairs, the eight individual persons. This is the Saṅgha of the Buddha's disciples that is worthy of offerings dedicated to the gods, worthy of hospitality, worthy of a religious donation, worthy of greeting with joined palms, and is the supreme field of merit for the world."- Nivesakasutta, AN 3.75

Among spiritual friends, some of you likely wished to experience nibbana, but the wish likely remained a mere wish, and you didn't find anyone who could explain to you the universal noble path common to all, and how you can correct your wrong views, misunderstandings, and how to train the mind in the middle way to understand beyond conventions, rituals and social practices or the path that goes beyond flood.

Now the noble path, rare to hear, is revealed to you. You may develop wholesome intentions based on right view: self and others are not stable, and thus, doing what is possible and making the most of what is left is wise, while ensuring not to hurt self or others. You can train yourself to consciously reduce grasping fetters, meaning let go of self-view and social practices by applying wisdom in daily life. You may associate with noble friends to receive support from nature's way. In this way, to develop noble wisdom, you may combine both conscious efforts and nature's way in the middle way.

Chapter 12
Losses and the common mode

To develop the noble path, when you experience losses and when expectations fail, if you experience sadness or overly worry, understand that your mind functions in the common mode; the way that you have been told to think since childhood. Since birth, a person has been told to think and made to understand that they should fulfil expectations, so that things should happen as a person likes, and that failure to do so is a cause for worry, and so on. Thus, when your mind functions in the common mode, understand that it works in the common way; a way that is not always true in line with life experience, a way that weakens happiness and peace, and gradually get rid of weakness by understanding it with wisdom as it happens during waking hours, to renounce suffering.

If your thoughts work in the common mode but you understand these words with wisdom, you have only heard Dhamma (first stage). Then, if you were to understand your thoughts functioning in common ways as they evolve while doing usual activities, understand that you are investigating the self (second stage). Then, in this manner, if you consistently apply wisdom in the middle way to reduce suffering arise in your thoughts within usual activities, understand you are training to let go of the fetters (social practices, and conventional understanding of self), and are working towards the noble path (third stage). Then, if your mind experiences peace and happiness naturally over time at some point, without having to consciously investigate or apply anything, and it works beyond common ways with wisdom with stability, you will understand that you experience Sotapanna as it evolves (ending of ordinary mind state).

> "What is abstruse, subtle, deep, hard to see, going against the flow; conventional understanding of self based on common ways, social practices, and alike — those delighting in such worldly experiences grounded on delusion, cloaked in the mass of darkness, won't see."- Ayacana Sutta, SN 6.1

Among spiritual friends, some of you likely wished to experience nibbana but did not get to hear about the direct practices, the universally applicable noble path, from anyone, or rarely. Now the direct practices, the universally applicable noble path, are revealed to you, and you may test the practice.

> "Together with one's attainment of insight, three qualities have been abandoned, namely: self-view, doubt and dependence on rites, ceremonies and conventions."- Ratana Sutta

Some people refer to Sotapanna as part of early Buddhist teachings, suggesting that there are later Buddhist teachings. Whenever you get to such things, you may correct your understanding; there is one universal Buddha. There is one universal Dhamma for all. There are four types of noble Sangha: Sotapanna, Sakadagami, Anagami, and Arahant. Anything other than Sotapanna, Sakadagami, Anagami, or Arahant is not the teachings of the Buddha but the teachings of ordinary people; those who do not represent the four stages are not the natural or universal disciples of the Buddha, and this summarizes a key aspect of the Universal Dhamma. The rest is what people have made up; you may want to think again if you want to enhance your well-being through understanding the noble truths. Conventional monks or conventional householders are in the early phase, during which a person first hears about Dhamma or comes to know and practice the very basics. Sotapanna and Sakadagami are the first phases of experience towards universal Dhamma, as they are more alike than not. Anagami is the middle phase of experience towards universal Dhamma. Arahant is the final phase of experience towards universal Dhamma. To experience the Sotapanna stage, you might initially train the mind to let go of the first three fetters by applying wisdom. There are many things people who have experienced Arahantship can tell you that are not mentioned in ancient books, practical things. You may develop wholesome intentions based on right view: self and others are not stable, and thus, doing what is possible and making the most of what is left is wise, while ensuring not to hurt self or others.

Chapter 13
Purpose

The purpose of Buddha's Dhamma is to extinguish mental sufferings with stability and to enhance well-being through enhancing both materially and spiritually at the Sotapanna state.

> "When someone grows in noble right view and noble ethics, wisdom, and both generosity and understanding life experience— a noble person such as one sees clearly, and in this very life one grows in both ways."- Vaḍḍhisutta, AN 10.74

When Buddha explained Dhamma, those who did not understand Dhamma and those who refused (eg. MN 87) Dhamma continued to experience mental suffering and samsara. When Buddha explained Dhamma, those who understood it were able to let go of mental suffering with stability.

> 'Sir, who on earth could ever think such a thing! For our loved ones bring us joy and happiness.' Disagreeing with what the Buddha said, rejecting it, he got up from his seat and left..."- Piyajātikasutta, MN 87

> "Associating with noble friends; people of noble linage one would be released from all suffering & stress, would know stress, the origination of stress, cessation & the noble eightfold path."- Thig 10, Kīsā Gotamī

There are many ways (i.e, common ways) you can reduce stress; you may go for a walk, do exercise, meet up with friends, travel the world, attend parties, meditate, or live a ritualistic lifestyle, but the satisfaction you can gain through common ways is subject to change. Thus, the remarkable things about nibbana that lie beyond common ways, a natural happening at a random time (universal happening), and it allows you to let go of stress with stability. You may adopt both common and noble ways to let go of mental stress until you experience the Anagami state, as after that, you would not need common ways to experience peace and happiness within. Some people may think you have to stop doing things you like or enjoy to experience Sotapanna, yet, if you were to interpret accurately as described by the Buddha, Dhamma is not what you do, but what you intentionally do or what you understand about what you do in life. You don't have to stop what you enjoy doing, but understand that what you do is subject to change in the middle way meaning things you enjoy only cut off to make sure you don't hurt others, but protect their dignity and rights.

Sometimes people can do unwholesome things without intending to, due to circumstances. Given the intention is karma, circumstances won't necessarily be a barrier to the universal noble path. The path is compassionate toward all beings; this is a perfect quality of the Buddha's universal Dhamma.

"...The bhikkhus then asked the Buddha, "Venerable Sir, is the wife of the hunter who is a sotapanna, also not guilty of taking life, if she has been getting things like nets, bows and arrows for her husband when he goes out hunting?" To this question the Buddha answered, "Bhikkhus, the sotapannas do not kill, they do not wish others to get killed. The wife of the hunter was only obeying her husband in getting things for him. Just as the hand that has no wound is not affected by poison, so also, because she has no intention to do evil she is not doing any evil..."- Dhp 124

"...The ordinary bhikkhus wondered how such an evil-doer could have such great benefit to experience Sotapanna after listening to the Dhamma just once...."- Dhp 100

When ordinary monks and nuns don't understand Sotapanna or nibbana through experience, it is difficult for them to interpret Dhamma accurately. Not interpreting Dhamma accurately leads to developing wrong views, preventing nibbana. Thus, there is a need to aid them in developing right view, so they can learn how to interpret Dhamma in line with the four stages of nibbana without misrepresenting Buddha's Dhamma. The same can be said regarding spiritual friends in any setting, and these words are shared with immense loving kindness merely to reveal the universal noble path, not to dislike any individual as a person. The purpose of universal Dhamma is not to become a conventional monk, conventional householder, or even to become an Arahant or Buddha, but to let go of mental sufferings in a stable manner and to end Samsara. The process of ending suffering in the mind by letting go of ten fetters is what we refer to as the four stages of Dhamma. You've known the basics for a long time, and you may understand beyond the basics to experience Sotapanna.

With regard to training, let go of first fetters including the self-view. To do that understand uncertainty related to self and worldly experiences; and apply wisdom to make the most of life while ensuring you do not hurt yourself or another to your level best within daily life. Understand that what you expect and what you don't expect can both happen. Understand that what you don't expect can happen is normal. When what you expected didn't happen, you were likely to get upset, worried, and anxious. Now shift that phase of self to become someone who understands life better and adopt a new way of facing life's experiences. When expectations fall off, instead of becoming sad or upset, try to take it easy without taking them too seriously, and don't let it make your mind feel heavy by understanding that it's part of life. Instead, devote more attention to resolving problems to your ability. Understand, as expectations fall, there is no point in regret; it's unwise to feel sad over things that didn't happen. It's already happened; it cannot be changed. Becoming sad is unpleasant, hurting yourself, and not worth it when you know life is short and passing away anyway; let it go instantly, wisely, and just because life passes away doesn't mean you should not enjoy things; instead, enjoy things, but don't get attached or magnify the things you enjoy (or not enjoy) with delusion while recalling the infinite wisdom and qualities in the universal Buddha, universal Dhamma or universal Sangha. If you can, constantly work on letting go of the first three fetters while reflecting on the universally applicable Triple Gem during day and night, there is no Dhamma training beyond this to experience Sotapanna.

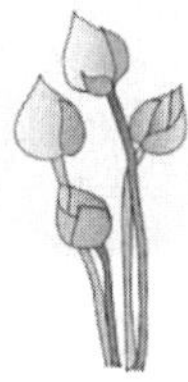

Chapter 14
Transformation

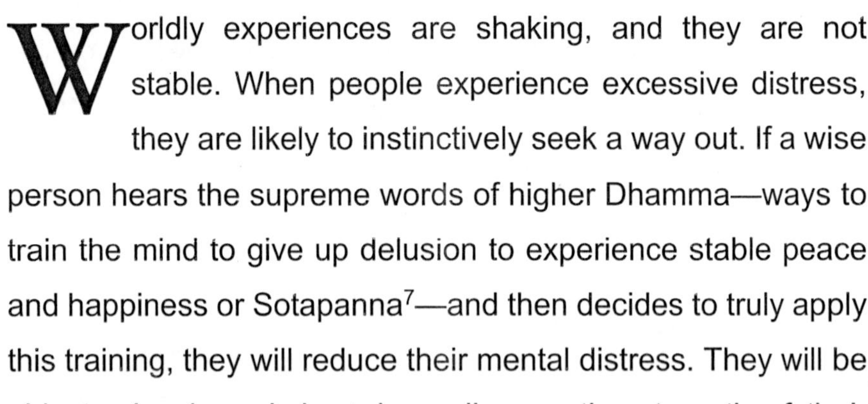

Worldly experiences are shaking, and they are not stable. When people experience excessive distress, they are likely to instinctively seek a way out. If a wise person hears the supreme words of higher Dhamma—ways to train the mind to give up delusion to experience stable peace and happiness or Sotapanna[7]—and then decides to truly apply this training, they will reduce their mental distress. They will be able to develop wisdom depending on the strength of their practice and experience stable peace and happiness through Sotapanna within.

There are things you can see. There are things you can't see. There are things you can hear. There are things you can't hear. There are things you understand through sensory information. There are things you can understand beyond sensory information with wisdom. To develop supreme wisdom

[7] From the outside, a Sotapanna will appear pleasant, childlike, due to having given up a few attachments, honest, and smiley; it's as if they are frozen in a happy world, day and night. However, merely looking outside must be avoided; instead, a person's understanding of Sotapanna that goes beyond conventions reflected in the way they explain nibbana is an indication of their understanding or experience of nibbana.

through noble view, you need to transcend whatever you think of yourself in your understanding (regardless of what others understand of you or see from a conventional point of view; monk, mother, father, sister, writer), and likewise.

You may let go of the deluded understanding of self (and other fetters) based on the universal truth; conventions are what you think as they exist with an underlying tendency to think they are stable, yet, worldly experiences are subject to change for everyone, universally applicable. Then, train your mind to apply wisdom to what you can do, instead of overly worrying about changing worldly experiences. If someone decides to apply words of higher Dhamma that transcend self-view and social practices to their spiritual practice, they will, as a consequence, experience their suffering subsiding. In addition, you may remind yourself that anyone can explain common things, but to explain something beyond common, that's something explained by the Buddhas. So, when true Buddhas appear, they explain something beyond common and social truths.

As you train to Sotapanna, bear in mind a few things: you are trying to discover universal truths explained by the Buddha applicable to all, the training path is the same for all. It is not merely a social truth, no difference in training for spiritual friends in monasteries and homes.

Grasping worldly experience in one way. Refusing worldly experiences is another way. To develop the middle way, you may give up grasping conventions, or refuse conventions; instead, let them be as they are, but don't give too much importance to such things or develop the delusion that such things are stable.

You may remind yourself that nibbana or Sotapanna is about emptiness- there is no person type, gender type, country or tradition type, clothing type, age type, caste type, or particular shape. Instead, it's an understanding (i.e. noble view or right view) that each person can experience within. Just as each person understands self, others, and the world, each person comes to understand the emptiness of self, and of social practices, rituals, and doubts, to begin with. Experiencing "noble right view" in your mental continuum is noble concentration for each person.

> "And how does unyoking come about? A woman doesn't focus on her own femininity.
>
> A man doesn't focus on his own masculinity: masculine moves, masculine appearance, masculine ways, masculine desires, masculine voice, and masculine adornment. He isn't stimulated by this and takes no pleasure in it..."- Saṁyogasutta, AN 7.51
>
> "...Friends, you're measured against what you have an underlying tendency for, and you're reckoned by what you're measured against..."
> - Dutiyaaññatarabhikkhusutta, SN 22.36

What you've commonly heard are the basic practices: Dana (giving and sharing), Sila (ethics), and Bavana (developing focus on the mind), but you've not commonly heard is how to train the mind beyond the basics to let go of deluded understanding of self and worldly experiences, and if you are interested in reducing mental distress in a stable manner and to make progress in the noble path, try to train your mind to find peace even in non-peaceful contexts. To do that, understand that experiencing non-peaceful situations is simply part of life, then understand that your understanding can change until you experience Sotapanna. Yet continue to shape understanding both through conscious efforts and by reflecting on the Triple Gem.

Based on ordinary view, one may interpret giving "Dana" as sharing random words of Dhamma or explaining them loosely without any reference to four stages of nibbana. However, giving "Dana" in line with the noble path means sharing the noble view that helps others develop right view, facilitating their entry into the universal noble path by allowing them to correct their vision, let go of non-noble or wrong views. To get there is a specific path across four stages universally applicable to all; developing wisdom to understand beyond self, rituals, conventions, and universal Triple Gem to begin with.

Chapter 15
Train out of context

If you happen to train your mind to find peace only in a peaceful context, it will be difficult to find it in a disturbing context. Then you will struggle in real life to maintain a stable peace; thus, know that it is a weak training of the mind, not quite strong enough to practice experiencing stable peace as yet, or nibbana. That's why, on the noble path, we always recommend you train to maintain peace in non-peaceful times.

Dependent peace is measurable. Freedom from dependent peace leads to experience immeasurable peace. If you wish to let go of mental distress in a stable manner and to make progress in the noble path, try to train your mind to find peace even in non-peaceful contexts. To do that, understand that experiencing non-peaceful situations is simply part of life, and recognizing this is the key to sharpening your wisdom.

When you experience problems in life, understand that engaging in resolving problems and situations is wise, and what is wise is wholesome. However, getting overly distressed drains your energy and can prevent you from working on finding solutions, which is unwholesome. In this way, try to train the mind to be wholesome and to give up unwholesome things when you first start practicing the noble path.

Through your personal experience, you would know that a mind has the ability to roam around, touch the world again and again, develop delusion and has the capability to like (greed based on delusion) or dislike (hate) things both in the presence or absence of things, people and alike. Try and train your mind to experience peace regardless of circumstances and independent of context can help you experience Sotapanna.

If you train external things but don't train the mind in the way you should, you are not training to noble path. Initially, you may train the mind to understand your thoughts as they maintain deluded understanding of self in your understanding within usual activities so that you don't need to separate practicing Dhamma from your usual activities. If you have to put conscious efforts and physically isolate yourself from usual activities to be able to concentrate and understand the impermanent nature of self, and to apply wisdom to experience the best of the world, it is an indication of a mind that has higher degree of deluded understand of self. By understanding your mind, you can train to progress in your mind.

> "Whether walking or standing, sitting or lying down, if you have the deluded understanding of self-view, social practices and other fetters (coming from sensory information), you're on the wrong path, lost

> among things that delude. Such a person is incapable of experiencing the highest awakening across stages. But one who, whether standing or walking, sitting or lying down, has come to understand delusion about self and other fetters in their thoughts, experiencing stable peace of mind; such a person is capable of experiencing the highest stage of awakening that comes after Sotapanna (or happy mind state)." - Carasutta, AN 4.11

In general, most spiritual friends throughout these centuries have sought nibbana in things outside their thoughts, and their mental continuum. That is the non-noble way. Instead, you may spend more time understanding yourself as thoughts occur. You may apply wisdom to make the best for the world while going about your usual activities. In doing so, you may shape your understanding to enter the noble path. Understand that uncertainty is the nature of worldly experience for all. Then if you were to apply wisdom, you will understand that getting over distress about uncertain things is not wise; ignorance is not wise. Thus, you may train to experience the world in the middle way based on the noble view.

Noble view is in harmony with true life experience. The noble view is that there are certain things you can make happen. There are things that happen as they happen. Thus, if you were to think all things should happen according to what you like or expect, understand it is unwise to think so, and maintain that understanding in your thoughts during waking hours as much as possible to develop noble concentration based on noble view.

Delusion means that when you experience displeasure, you have an underlying tendency to expect it to be otherwise in every thought during waking hours by nature. Sotapanna means when you experience displeasures, you know without a doubt that what you experience is what is normal life experience, nothing unusual, to be shocked or upset about it in mind, instead do what you can do to resolve it without overly getting distressed about it, making the best of worldly experiences based on wisdom. Understanding the differences in these mind states, you may continue to enhance happiness and peace in your mind and mental continuum by applying wisdom in daily life.

Chapter 16
Noble living

There are two ways to live life; one is the ordinary way to live life, touching worldly experiences coming from sensory information again and again in the mind as if they are too important, too valuable, with an underlying tendency to think they are stable, the standard way everyone follows since birth, and the other is the noble way of life.

What is ordinary life?

Ordinary life is shaped by social practices and routines, where most people tend to think themselves are stable (based on delusion). On the other hand, the noble path is developing noble wisdom to understand beyond the self-view and social practices, and at least to experience Sotapanna.

What you know is the ordinary mind. What you do not know is the noble mind state, or Sotapanna. It's something you are trying to discover. To discover the noble mind state within yourself, you may ask wise questions. Self-guided discovery can help you reduce mental strains coming from life's pressures. Since ups and downs are a natural part of everyone's life, when life's difficulties arise, instead of becoming overly sad, ask yourself, "why am I becoming sad?".

When you reflect on this, you may find two viable answers: you feel sad because you have an underlying expectation that certain things should not happen as the way they happen, or because you have strong likes or dislikes regarding certain experiences. Once you find these answers, take a further step to question yourself: "what made me think that sad things shouldn't happen, but in reality, anything can happen in life?". The answer lies in the misguided understanding of life, which leads a person to expect that things should unfold exactly as they wish. In this way, you can lead yourself to discovery by asking questions about yourself, reflecting on yourself and sharpening your wisdom through self-questioning. You may check on your prior understandings to see if they are still acceptable by applying wisdom. For instance, you may question whether wisdom can be gained through attire or merely through rituals. If you answered that rituals alone can make a person let go of grasping self-view and social practices, then that is lacking wisdom. By questioning, understanding, and identifying where you lack wisdom, you can fill the gaps and enhance your wisdom.

In this manner, you may investigate deep into your understanding of self and universal Dhamma with wisdom. As you train to develop the noble path, your mind should reduce delusion, unwise thinking ways, jealousy, pride, need to compare one another as people, need to pretend (for example, to act as if you know all about nibbana until you experience the stages of nibbana), and likewise.

Remember that it is likely that if you were to spend too much time looking into others, you would have less time to understand yourself and your thoughts beyond self-view and social practices. Thus, spiritual friends who aspire to growth on the noble path may take extra time to deepen their understanding of the self and worldly experiences beyond the fetters, address the root cause of suffering, delusion. You may apply wisdom to reflect on life experience, grow in understanding it, and transform into a wiser person with noble qualities.

If you are touching your worldly experiences again and again; likes, dislikes, too many expectations based on delusion, chances are you will likely suffer within. To develop the noble path, you may reduce the deluded understanding of worldly experiences in daily life. If you happen to maintain an underlying tendency to think that self and worldly experiences are stable, and that social practices are very much important in your mental continuum, if you are wise, you should be able to understand that you have lived and are living an ordinary life, regardless of whether you reside in a monastery or at home.

> "Friends, I don't praise wrong practice for these two, for spiritual friends who live in homes and monasteries. Because of wrong practice, neither for

> spiritual friends who live in homes and monasteries succeed in completing the system of the skillful teaching.
>
> I praise right practice for these two, for spiritual friends who live in homes and monasteries. Because of right practice, spiritual friends who live in homes and monasteries succeed in completing the system of the skillful teaching."- AN 2.40 (Samacittavagga)

When you live an ordinary life, chances are you will likely to get too much unpleasantness through worldly experiences. If you seek a way out, depending on your level of wholesome (Kusala) and wisdom, you will be able to see for yourself, understanding yourself by reflecting on yourself and your worldly experiences beyond self-view and other fetters in daily life.

In general, some spiritual friends misunderstand and think engaging in rituals is the path to Sotapanna. Instead, it should be understood that developing wisdom to seek universal truth within is the path to Sotapanna. As it's a path within, outside does not matter. A person may live wherever, dress however, and eat whatever, as these things don't directly affect a person's understanding of life as unstable and lacking stable satisfaction due to its changing nature. Then, if you were to question, why has no one told you before that outside does not matter, but inside is what matters for the path? It's because you heard from those who shaped only the outside but didn't know how to shape understanding within to experience nibbana.

When you seek truth, you take on false things; no matter what you do, you can't experience truth. In any case, an outside world can only be understood from within. Thus, you should now understand that the path to Sotapanna is about developing wise understanding within. If a person has an underlying tendency to think that worldly experiences are stable, to feel pride, to harbor ill will, or to give too much value to social practices that lead to grasping or fuel within, they are failing the noble path, regardless of whether one lives in a monastery or at home. That's why it's explained that one must follow the precise training path to experience the four stages of Dhamma.

If you tend to think worldly experiences are stable, and give too much value to your worldly experiences, chances are you are likely to suffer from your mental continuum. As you suffer within, you should understand that is ordinary mind or ordinary life, not the true path to freedom from mental distress or the noble way of living life. The noble way of living leads to understanding universal truths, the true path to the Sotapanna. To interpret precisely as interpreted by the Buddha, renounce, is a mind state- a state where deluded understanding or the ten fetters are gone across four stages of nibbana.

Learn about the noble path with accuracy, not loosely. What is not possible for a Sotapanna is to misinterpret the universal Dhamma by explaining it as merely convention or social practice, rituals, or traditions. They will also avoid the six major wrong doings.

> "Together with one's attainment of insight, three qualities have been abandoned, namely: wrong belief in selfhood, doubt and dependence on social practices, rites and ceremonies and grasping conventions. One is absolutely freed from the four states of misery, and is incapable of commiting the six major wrong doings. In the universal Sangha is this precious jewel found. On account of this truth, may there be well-being!" -Ratana Sutta

To commence the noble practice and fruition, you may develop supreme wisdom to understand life experience in your mental continuum and develop noble qualities across the four-fold nibbana. Once you decide to follow the noble path, try not to touch worldly experiences again and again in an unwholesome manner, instead understand what is wholesome, and what is unwholesome in the middle way. Once you have completed the perfect training path that does not hurt oneself or others, you may invite fellow spiritual friends who seek an escape from distress to test the practice.

Chapter 17
Not outside but inside you

Dhamma is something you have to develop within. One easy way to develop the noble path is to let go of restricted thinking based on common ways[8]. This can be explained as follows: you learned to think there is a stable self and that you should receive things you like, and have your expectations fulfilled, and so on, based on common ways and social practices since birth. Yet as you continue to live your life, you are likely to experience hurt, disappointments, frustrations, and mental distress while thinking in line with what society says or common social practices. When you realised life brings mental distress, if you were wise, it is likely that you thought it was not worth the pain, and likely you were seeking ways to let go of distress. If you want to let go of distress and are seeking a way out, you may try to train yourself to think beyond common ways.

In general, when you get things you like, you become happy; when you lose things, you tend to become sad, and likewise. When you experience pleasant things, you will anyway remain pleasant in mind. To train to noble path, train to

[8] Common ways refer to giving too much value to standard social practices.

give up dual mind state. To do that, when you experience unpleasant things, try and find pleasant things in them by understanding that it is not worth experiencing unpleasantness in changing worldly experience, as they are changing anyway, a natural process. In this way, as you experience both pleasant and unpleasant worldly experiences, try and train to maintain a pleasant mind, a peaceful mind state that is wise and not dependent on worldly experience based on delusion. When you escape dual worldly experiences through the wisdom-based middle mind, you can instantly reduce suffering arising from worldly experiences. Middle way means wholesome way. In other words, you need to be able to do wholesome things (i.e. resolving things that need resolving) and cut off unwholesome things (excessively worries etc.) to develop wisdom based middle way. When you apply wisdom to think beyond and in contrast to social practices, initially you may experience some difficulties, yet as you encounter difficulties, if you continue to train yourself not to touch the difficulties again and again in your mind, you are training your mind to let go of attachment to the world.

> "The non-doing of anything unwholesome in intentional actions, undertaking of what is wholesome in intentional actions, this is the teaching of the Buddhas."- Dhp 183

Sotapanna or nibbana is about developing wholesomeness within you. Whatever hurts you is non-dhamma. When you maintain non-dhamma within you, it can hurt you, another person, or both. When you let go of non-dhamma by taking in Dhamma, you don't hurt yourself or others. In this manner, you may develop Dhamma within to experience the wholesome. Greed, hate, and delusion is non-dhamma. Maintaining greed or excessive likes to worldly experiences arising from sensory information is maintaining non-dhamma. Maintaining dislikes or hate towards self or others, dividing and treating people differently based on social practices, is maintaining non-dhamma. The underlying tendency to think that the self and others are stable and to give too much value or importance to worldly experiences based on sensory information and expectations is maintaining non-dhamma. You may let go of non-dhamma within you to let go of mental distress through both conscious efforts and nature's way[9] in the middle way.

You may initially take refuge in the universal Triple Gem to find refuge in yourself, independent and free at the Arahant stage. This explains why Dhamma should be taken as a raft. First, you need to learn the basics. Thereafter, you have to dive beyond the basics to let go of them and progress through the stages. In this manner, Dhamma is progressive. Thus, the path to Sotapanna begins with understanding beyond the self-view, social practices, and the universal Triple Gem within.

[9] Nature's way refers to associating with the universal Triple Gem.

What you think as "you" is created, maintained, and transformed as a rhythm; a cyclic pattern of breathing again and again, eating again and again while living and so on, thoughts coming and going while living, taking a new body again and again in samsara is within the nature or universe. The universe knows what is created, maintained, "cycled, and recycled" within the universe, and those who have purified through paramis and are letting go of the ten fetters across stages, are transformed into the emptiness of nature without having to bear another body after the death of their physical body. Bearing a body as a separate person in the universe means one has to face the unlimited universal rhythm within the limited or restricted body, mind, and sensory information, and life becomes suffering.

> "This transmigration has no known beginning. No first point is found of sentient beings roaming and transmigrating, shrouded by ignorance and fettered by craving. "- Tiṁsamattasutta, SN 15.13

Universe functions in certain ways; so when you get close to fire, you get to experience heat and not cold, when you experience low temperatures you get to experience cold not heat. In the same way, when you initially seek refuge in those who have truly purified from delusion to worldly experiences in your mental continuum, the mirror image of such a purity will generate within you, and the energy transformation or purity is what you get to experience within you by nature, and this is a helpful practice until you experience the Anagami state. This explains why Buddha described himself as unique, special, and incomparable to any other person in the world, out of compassion for spiritual friends, as Buddha alone holds a unique position as the teacher of humans and gods. Thus, know precisely that whoever misinterprets universal Dhamma, and in doing so, asks you to go against the universal Buddha or ignores Buddha's unique position in the universal Dhamma, is driving you to develop a wrong view. Similarly, whoever ignores the noble Sangha's position in the process of nibbana is driving you to suffer.

> "For me, there is no teacher. One like me does not exist. In the world with its devas, there is no one who equals me."- Pāsarāsisutta, MN 26

The worldly experience coming from sensory information is created and understood not outside but within each person. The same object (i.e., a colourful ball) is seen differently and understood differently by a blind person or a person with poor vision and a good vision. At times, even the same words are understood differently by different people. Words are empty, and words including self, others, and the world are understood not outside but within each person. This explains why, the higher Dhamma related to the four stages of nibbana, can only be understood not outside but within you.

> "...The Buddha continued to stay there, near the brahmin couple for three more months and during that time, both the brahmin and his wife attained arahatship, and later passed away due to old age..."- Dhp 225

Some spiritual friends explain Dhamma loosely, without accurately describing it across the stages, and for example, some of them sometimes say that celibacy is an important aspect of Sotapanna; that is incorrect. The reason for this is that Sotapanna is to be developed through wisdom, not through sila. This explains why the sila-based path proposed by Devadatta was rejected by the Buddha. This aspect of universal Dhamma makes it unique and different from various other spiritual paths and conventional Dhamma practices. Try to understand Dhamma across stages with precision. This can be explained as follows. There are many spiritual paths and social practices, and celibacy is commonly adopted by many of them. Yet, Buddha's noble path is not common. Ananagami gives up sensual pleasures and the need to maintain celibacy through conscious effort. A Sotapanna may or may not maintain celibacy depending on personal choice, as they only give up lower fetters while retaining sensual fetters. Thus, to experience "Sotapanna" state in mind, you may cultivate wholesome deeds, especially the right view.

> "Those who refrain from killing living creatures, who refrain from stealing, who refrain from sexual misconduct, who refrain from lying, who refrain from

divisive speech, who refrain from harsh speech, who refrain from talking nonsense, are not covetous, are not malicious, have the right view with those who have the right view."- Dasakammapathasutta, SN 14.27

In conventional Dhamma practice, the basics are designed to sustain Dhamma through social practices from one generation to another, and for those who want to train over Samsara. On the other hand, nibbana is to end the continuation of Samsara for those who have completed paramis, and it brings the end of delusion regarding self-view, social practices, and other fetters, and the highest level of Buddha's Dhamma. Thus, don't misunderstand the basics and higher Dhamma as the same, as they are not. Instead, spiritual friends who are yet to experience Sotapanna in monasteries and homes, you may develop from the basics to higher stages of nibbana.

Chapter 18
Delusion

The path to delusion is an ordinary way. The ordinary way is that when a person has many things, yet they worry about a few they haven't got. Letting go of delusion is the path to Sotapanna. The ordinary way is to become unhappy over things that are lost, even if one has many things; the basics, such as food, accommodation, and sensory organs, are functioning to a reasonable level, and likewise. The Sotapanna's way is happy with everything and doesn't need anything further to be happy; a mental state. Thus, to become a Sotapanna, you may train your mind to be happy when you experience losses; that's a way of renouncing in the noble path.

To find happiness in loss, let's say you lose a job and instead of getting overly sad, try to find a reason why you can be happy; you may think that losing a job gives you extra free time to do things you like, or another opportunity to find something else, and so on. When you are happy to give up, grounded in wisdom, that's how you develop the wisdom-based path to stable happiness, or Sotapanna. If you take another example, if you happen to lose someone dear, instead of getting overly stressed, understand that losses are all part of life, and, if you've fulfilled your obligation to your dear one, find peace in that. This explains why a person who wants to find peace should always try to fulfil obligations to all, considering each moment spent with them precious, so that once they depart, you can find peace in the good deeds you have done. You may also try not to do things you regret later. In this manner, by applying the wisdom to do your best, not to hurt yourself, and not to hurt others, you can cultivate wholesome thoughts by letting go of self-view on the noble path.

When you experience the world through sense bases, you tend to experience distress and inner fires as long as you expect that everything you desire will happen (i.e., delusion), or have likes (i.e., greed) and dislikes (i.e., hate). Likes and dislikes alone do not necessarily cause distress but expecting what you like or dislike to happen does. In other words, delusions cause distress. Delusion is not in dress, food, lifestyle, or accommodation, but in the mind of a person. When a person has a delusion, whatever dress they wear, they still have a delusion. When a person has a delusion, whatever food they eat, they still retain the delusion. Typically, when you are in a good mood, you will see the beauty of good weather, and if in a bad mood, you will likely not notice or enjoy it. If you can understand your mood with wisdom and understand that every time you touch anything in worldly experience, it can produce inner fires, then learn how to live without causing fires by applying wisdom. People around the world know many things very well, but rarely do they know how to experience changing nature within without causing distress within, and to experience stable happiness and peace. And that's what is rarely known is discovered through the path to Sotapanna. If you use a paraphrase, the path to Sotapanna is like learning to eat delicious sweets or a cake in a way that's not going to make you put on fat or sick, in the sense that you learn to live life to the fullest while minimising unwholesome pain or distress coming from daily life experiences. Nibbana is in the nature; just as nature contributed to your experience of inner fires, you can learn how to cease such fires in line with universal laws.

Those who have less dust, or less greed, hate, and delusion, or a deluded understanding of self and social practices, are likely to associate with others who have similar qualities. Those who have too much greed, hate, and delusion are likely to associate those with those who have similar qualities.

> "...Lord, let the Blessed One teach the Dhamma! Let the One-Well-Gone teach the Dhamma! There are beings with little dust in their eyes who are falling away because they do not hear the Dhamma. There will be those who will understand the Dhamma..."- Ariyapariyesana Sutta,MN 26

In terms of practice, spiritual friends in monasteries and homes who have yet to experience the mind state of a

Sotapanna, they may engage in developing ten wholesome deeds, especially the noble understanding or right view.

> "...Friends, sentient beings join together and converge because of an element those who have wrong view join with those who have wrong view.
>
> Those who have no intention to killing living creatures, stealing, engaging in sexual misconduct, lying, speak divisively, speak harsh or talking things that are not relevant for the training path to Sotapanna, are not covetous, are not malicious, have the right view with those who have the noble or right view..."- Dasakammapathasutta, SN 14.27

One of the common ways of thinking and doing is to do things now with the anticipation of finding happiness in the future. Therefore, people may choose to do various things, such as meditating to find nibbana (stable happiness) in the future, studying now, or working hard now, with the hope that such efforts will lead to happiness in the future. Instead, you may choose to do what is beneficial while also maintaining happiness and peace within each moment, now, without waiting for the future. In general, people tend to associate with those who are similar to them. Those who like rituals embrace those who like rituals. Those who like meditations follow those who like meditations. Those who have the wisdom to understand life experience to a reasonable extent, the potential to see beyond self-view and social practices, (i.e Sotapanna), can understand when someone speaks wise words that go beyond self-view and social practices, the training path to Sotapanna.

> “...Sentient beings join together and converge because of an element: those who do not know about nibbana or Sotapanna through experience join with those who do not know Sotapanna through experience, lazy witless. The learned with the learned energetic wise...” - Appassutamūlakasutta, SN 14.21

> “Friends, sentient beings join together and converge because of an element: the faithless with the faithless, shameless with shameless, imprudent ...and the wise with the wise...”- Asamāhitasutta, SN 14.23

Nibbana, the path, and the Triple Gem are things you (or each person) should understand and develop within. In other words, Dhamma is not in words, as they are inherently empty but what each person understands in words. You may develop the stages of nibbana within.

> "And what, Ananda, is that teaching called the Mirror of Dhamma, possessing which the noble disciple may thus declare of oneself?

> In this case, Ananda, the noble disciple possesses experiential confidence in the universal Buddha thus: 'The Blessed One is an Arahant, the Fully Enlightened One, perfect in knowledge and conduct, the Happy One, the knower of the world, the paramount trainer of beings, the teacher of gods and men, the Enlightened One, the Blessed One.'

> One possesses experiential confidence in the universal Dhamma thus: 'Well propounded by the

Blessed One is the universal Dhamma, evident, timeless, inviting investigation, leading to emancipation, to be comprehended by the wise, each for himself.'

One possesses experiential confidence in the Blessed One's noble Order of universal Disciples thus: 'Well faring is the Blessed One's Order of universal Disciples, righteously, wisely, and dutifully: that is to say, the four pairs of persons (Sotapanna etc.), the eight classes of persons. The Blessed One's universal Sangha Order of Disciples is worthy of honor, of hospitality, of offerings, of veneration — the supreme field for meritorious deeds in the world.'

And one possesses noble virtues, complete and perfect, spotless and pure, which are liberating, praised by the supreme wise, uninfluenced (by worldly experience coming from sensory information), and favorable to concentration of mind based on right view.

This, Ananda, is the teaching called the Mirror of the Dhamma, whereby the noble disciple may thus know of oneself: 'There is no more rebirth for me in hell, nor as an animal or ghost, nor in any realm of woe. A stream-enterer am I, safe from falling into the states of misery, assured am I and bound for Enlightenment."- Mahāparinibbānasutta, DN 16

Chapter 19
Understanding the truths within

When you seek the universally applicable noble truths, remember that because you are a part of the universe and experience the universe within. Seeking universal truth means you are seeking truth in yourself. Thus, when you come to train the mind to seek universal truth through the noble path, you may avoid hiding your good, bad, ugly thoughts to yourself pretending to not know about such thoughts, or ignore, or hide your thoughts to yourself. Instead, take your thoughts as they are, without hiding but revealing to you, then reduce unwholesome thoughts to only those that hurt you or others in the middle way. When you deepen universal Dhamma within you, you also come to understand universal Buddha and universal Sangha within you.

Each person can understand another within their mind. An ordinary person understands Sotapanna within their mind. A Sotapanna understands an ordinary person within their own understanding, which explains why a Sotapanna can understand an ordinary person, but an ordinary person struggles to understand a Sotapanna. A Sotapanna understands the supreme Buddha within their understanding. An Arahant understands the supreme Buddha through four stages of Dhamma and Arahantship. Another supreme Buddha can completely understand supreme Buddha. In this manner, each person understands the Triple Gem within one's own understanding.

One way in which you can practice to experience Sotapanna for an ordinary person is by understanding how to make life experience blissful and not suffering. This can be explained as follows: if you were to think you are stable (delusion) and getting ill (getting poor, getting to experience problems of many kinds) is not normal(delusion), it can make you distressed. Yet if you were to think you are not stable (true life experience) and getting ill is normal (true life experience) and not too much bother about it (not attached in the middle way and apply wisdom- do what you can do to make things better and not bother about things you can't do) and do what you can do to make things resolve can make your life the best possible experience regardless of circumstances.

To understand universally applicable noble truths, one must be committed to investigating the truths. If applied truth, you would understand and agree that there is a danger in merely trying to understand Dhamma through hearing from those who are yet to understand Sotapanna within. Universal Dhamma is in-depth. Thus, it's easier to misunderstand the universal Dhamma and develop a wrong view that is not aligned with the noble view. Dhamma decline means people misinterpret the Dhamma.

When someone falsely declare Arahantship and declare Dhamma matters inaccurately that leads to harm. Thus, pay extra attention to how a person describes Dhamma. Memorizing discourses and performing rituals is not Sotapanna as an experience, but understanding self, worldly experiences as impermanent in every thought, and understanding of meaninglessness of clinging to social practices with and underlying tendency to think they are valuable, understanding what’s missing in discourses, ancient writings, and understanding what's missing in commonly spoken Dhamma matters is how you can develop an understanding of Sotapanna. In the way a person draws, sings, dances, and explains various subject matter, another person with some degree of sense can tell if that particular individual is good at drawing, dancing, and various other subjects. Similarly, when a person describes Dhamma, a person who knows about the four stages of the nibbana can easily identify misinterpretations and correct them to reveal the noble path and a person who has some degree of wisdom can understand the truth.

Characteristics of an ordinary person with no understanding of universal Dhamma are that they describe Dhamma in two extremes:

One should not declare Arahantship to be an extreme.

One should declare that Arahantship is another extreme.

Words are inherently empty, but how you understand words makes them alive or meaningful for you. The middle way means using words in a beneficial way, avoiding harm to yourself and others. Misinterpreting Dhamma is what is harmful, as it prevents the vision of a Sotapanna. Accurately explaining things related to the four stages of nibbana is beneficial. Those who know the middle way through personal experience of cessation, when they explain the middle way with accuracy without ego, expecting material or honors or special treatment (indicators of no greediness in their mind), without disliking anyone as a person (indicators of no hate), without misunderstanding self or worldly experience as stable in their thought with stability (no delusion), they represent higher Dhamma in the way it should be represent to the community of spiritual friends.

> "Friends, these five things lead to the decline and disappearance of the true teaching. What five?
>
> It's when the spiritual friends memorize discourses that they learned incorrectly, with misplaced words and phrases and misinterpretations. When the words and phrases are misplaced or misinterpreted, the meaning is misinterpreted.

> This is the first thing that leads to the decline and disappearance of the true teaching."- Tatiyasaddhammasammosasutta, AN 5.156

> "One should act as one teaches others; only with oneself thoroughly tamed should one tame other. To tame oneself is, indeed, difficult."- Dhp 159

Liking is one way of grasping worldly experiences. Disliking is another way of grasping worldly experiences. When you like worldly experiences, you have a world within your understanding. When you dislike worldly experience, you have a world within your understanding. Giving up both ways of grasping by cutting of the root or delusion, one can develop path to cessation across stages. Similarly, conventional monk is one way of grasping worldly experience coming from sensory information. Conventional householder is another way of grasping worldly experiences. Giving up both ways of grasping by cutting of the root or delusion, one can develop path to cessation across stages. If you are taking the truths as your foundation, you will understand that wherever you go, whatever you do, as long as you bear a body, you experience world. Practicing to Sotapanna means not giving up one worldly experience and taking another, but to understand whatever you experience as worldly through sensory information with wisdom. Nibbana is not merely in words but in what you understand within (or right view) words. This can be explained as below:

If you say there are conventional monks and conventional householders with an underlying tendency to think they are stable or attach too much importance, then there are things for you; delusion exists. An ordinary, wise person can understand impermanence, but they tend to forget. A Sotapanna can understand impermanence, but they can't forget the impermanent nature of self and worldly experience in changing thoughts, even if they try to do so through conscious efforts. This explains why to progress in the universal Dhamma, each person must develop understanding within and create a place where they can find refuge, a place away from the sufferings that come from worldly experiences.

To get there, initially, you may depend on the universal Triple Gem until the Anagami state, and thereafter, you become the Triple Gem within, at the Arahant state. At the Arahant state, when your deluded understanding of worldly experience ceases, and you can see your thoughts as they are in a separate sheet with wisdom, and without having to put any conscious effort, by nature. You may develop step by step across the stages of nibbana.

> "...Ānanda, it's not easy to teach from Sotapanna to Arahantship to others. Unless you establish five things in yourself, it is not appropriate to teach from Sotapanna to Arahantship to others.
>
> What five?

> You should teach Dhamma to others thinking: 'I will teach step by step across four stages of Nirvana Dhamma.'
>
> 'I will teach showing my method that I personally know.'
>
> 'I will teach out of immeasurable kindness.'
>
> 'I will not teach while secretly hoping to profit or gains for myself.'
>
> 'I will teach without hurting myself or others.'
>
> It's not easy to teach higher Dhamma to others. You should establish these five things in yourself before teaching Dhamma to others…" - Udāyīsutta, AN 5.159

Among the community of spiritual friends, a very few of you know nibbana for yourself, and others may develop their understanding across the stages. We who understand nibbana for ourselves and represent Buddha's higher Dhamma are not here to show off "I am this and that" or to downgrade another at individual level or as a person (i.e., intentional action) but to clarify misunderstandings and purify the right understanding of the higher Dhamma, merely for the purpose of helping the community of friends to escape mental suffering in a stable manner with immeasurable loving kindness.

Chapter 20
Surpassing conventional paths with wisdom

Discuss below is how you can develop wisdom based on understanding the universally applicable noble truths.

Going with social practices and what is valued by society is living with conventions. The conventional path involves arranging necessities that support living, such as earning a livelihood, securing accommodation or shelter, clothing, and social relationships, including interacting with associates, including shaping external factors. Noble path means understanding the instability of self, social practices to begin with. The noble path is about discovering the truth about the root cause of suffering (i.e, delusion) that lies beyond self-view and conventions, regardless of external factors. First, to discover the truths, be willing to openly explore yourself and reveal yourself to yourself in order to understand the truths. If society says something is valuable, if your mind or an untrained mind tends to grasp or adopt what is valued by society; understand that is how you go with the flow (ordinary or "anariyan way") or the conventional path. Instead, you may surpass or understand beyond what value by the common social practices is to understand the universally applicable noble truths.

People tend to understand themselves, others, and the world through conventions since birth. You are being trained to be happy when you gain things you like and to become sad when you lose things, based on social practices and conventions. Then, when a person continues to follow the standard way, at some point, if you realise you suffer, you may try the noble way. For example, when you encounter difficult situations and problems in real life, the standard way is to make a problem or difficult situation too much of a problem in your mind. It means getting sad or upset or distressed by thinking about the distressing situation again and again. Instead, to follow the noble path, divert your complete attention to find a remedy for the situation. If explained by a mathematical equation, your problem should be equivalent to finding a solution in your mind.

Problem= finding solutions

This is one way in which you can renounce sufferings come from "self-view" with wisdom in the noble path.

When you hear these words, yet you continue to give too much value for conventions because, for you, they are very important, your value for conventions prevents you from experiencing Sotapanna. Instead, you may awaken your wisdom to understand beyond conventions. Remember to follow the noble path; a prerequisite is that you have a higher degree of wisdom to surpass common ways. Also, your willingness and courage to understand the truths for yourself. As it's a path that surpasses conventions, you need to be able to surpass the majority's views or stand with superior wisdom in the crowd that goes with the flood, to not go with it. Understanding beyond the majority, you isolate yourself in the path leading to wisdom. That is how you renounce on the noble path. You isolate yourself not because you dislike others, but because you have developed superior wisdom, which is difficult to discern from sensory information alone. First, you may develop wisdom and after you experience the four stages of nibbana, or Sotapanna share it with those who seek liberation through superior wisdom with immeasurable loving kindness.

A person tends to create an idea of a stable self from childhood, based on social learning. Thus, chances are, even when you don't want or don't know, your mind may have a tendency to act like a puppet who merely goes with the flow. Instead, understand how socially created information or data, and social practices, only reveal partial life experience, and there are things that goes beyond social practices. By awakening wisdom and letting go of delusion, you may be able to release suffering while also enjoying social practices, experiencing the best of the conventional and spiritual life through worldly experiences.

To develop the noble path, one must learn to develop truthfulness and speak the truth and revel the truth. Speaking the truth, whoever prioritizes standing by social practices tends to lose sight of the noble path. Unlike in Buddha's time, these days hearing the true version of Sotapanna is rare. Instead, there is a strong market for meditation classes or retreats in today's context, and it has become a way of making gains for some spiritual practitioners. Even without a person's knowing, if someone happens to have the intention or thought of using the Dhamma to make a living, that itself will steal away your ability to experience renunciation of gains for self and the noble path.

The sole purpose of Dhamma should be to seek refuge to end suffering. The path explains how an ordinary person can take refuge in the universal Triple Gem to develop a mirror of Dhamma, and the Triple Gem within to find a refuge in self across the stages of nibbana. When you seek universal truths within, it is important to avoid misunderstanding that common meditation classes are a means to experience Sotapanna or nibbana. Instead, understand life experience with wisdom. Whoever prioritizes common way of understanding self will continue to carry the burden of self. Instead, when you prioritize Dhamma (i.e., noble way of understanding self), when you find yourself as a place where you can take refuge by applying Dhamma and when you and Dhamma become one, you can overcome the self-view that bothers the self the most across the stages of nibbana.

Training path to nibbana refers to understanding the impermanent nature[10] of the self, others, and the world through the ten fetters. An ordinary, wise person can understand impermanence, but they tend to forget. A Sotapanna can understand impermanence, but they can't forget the impermanent nature of self and worldly experience in changing thoughts, even if they try to do so through conscious efforts. Once your mind gets on the path of nibbana, you can only progress; there is no downward movement. Therefore, those who feel they have had enough of suffering in worldly experiences stemming from sensory experiences may apply the practice to reduce grasping self-view and other fetters within daily life.

Buddhahood is a state of understanding that transcends the self-view and conventions (other fetters), characterized by wisdom in daily life. Among spiritual friends in monasteries (or homes), you may remind yourself that you are not living a conventional lifestyle for the sake of living a lifestyle or to

---

[10]In addition, understanding dissatisfaction arising from the changing nature.

understand limited social truths, but to understand yourself and the universal truths for the purpose of letting go of mental sufferings coming from sensory information with stability. If you intend to follow the universal Buddha's path, it's beneficial to remind yourself that one cannot have hidden motives or need to pretend to know all about Dhamma and explain other things that you don't know or embrace mere rituals, as the universe knows what's within, it can produce mirror-like consciences prolonging sufferings. To avoid that, one may carefully examine one's thoughts and let go of impurities.

One simple way in which you can purify yourself is not addressing yourself and fellow ordinary monks or nuns as "venerable" as it's an utter misinterpretation of universal Dhamma or mind states or Sangha. The declaration of "venerable" or "holy" mind states should come only after a purified mind, and purified from what? A mind that is purified by not grasping self, conventions, and other fetters. Misrepresenting the universal Dhamma and universal Sangha is like touching a sharp double-edged sword that is about to injure you in many ways, and avoiding misrepresentation supports your own progress in the noble path.

To understand your mind states, you may think and analyse as follows: if you think there are conventional monks and conventional householders with an underlying tendency to think they are stable or attach too much importance, then there are things for you; delusion exists. If those who experience Arahantship say there are Arahants and ordinary people, knowing both are subject to decay, and merely use words to explain the Dhamma without needing to compare themselves and others as individuals, then there are no things for them - delusion has been given up. If your mind has a tendency to think “I'm great”, “I’m this” based on conventions with an underlying tendency to thinks elf is stable - that is developing self-view, which is the path that takes you away from the noble path. Instead, if you have a mind that completely understands the impermanent nature of self and others in changing thoughts with stability (i.e. Sotapanna), even if you use mere words such as “I am this or that”, such words are merely explaining Dhamma and are empty of delusion for you. If you have a mind that completely understands the impermanent nature of self and others as well as dissatisfaction coming from sensory information in changing thoughts with stability (i.e. Anagami), even if you use mere words such as “I am this or that”, such words are merely explaining Dhamma and are empty of delusion for you. In this manner, nibbana is not merely in words but in what you understand within words.

> “One who does not possess four things is said to have fallen from this Dhamma and discipline. What four? (1) One who does not possess noble virtuous behavior (i.e. Sotapanna) is said to have fallen from this Dhamma and discipline...

> "But, friends, one who possesses four things is said to be secure in this Dhamma and discipline. What four? (1) One who possesses noble virtuous behavior is said to be secure in this Dhamma and discipline…" - Papatitasutta, AN 4.2

In the noble path, one cannot hide and seek, and one must develop truthfulness and non-harming both towards self and others. Those who have delusions about self and conventions tend to have delusions about Sotapanna or nibbana.

If you would like to progress toward letting go of mental distress in a stable manner, or toward Sotapanna, be vigilant of your mind states and engage in ten wholesome deeds (dasa kusal), especially by developing the right view[11].

[11] You can develop the right view by associating with the spiritual friends who represent the universally applicable Buddha, Dhamma, and Sangha.

Chapter 21
Evidence-based wisdom

Understand Sotapanna or nibbana is something you have to develop through understanding life experiences with wisdom. As you let go of delusion, too much liking (greediness) and hate (dislikes) based on delusion, or an underlying tendency to think oneself is stable, you should be able to reduce fires within. To achieve that, you may simply learn to apply wisdom in daily life.

If you were to think all that you expect should happen, that's delusion. When you understand that and let go of that, it's practicing wisdom-based nobility. If you were to think that those who you like and are dear to you should always be there for you, but at any time, when they are not there for you, let that go instantly, as letting go of expectations grounded on delusion is renouncing in the universal path. As you let go of delusion, your suffering will cease, and it will become evident to you.

Letting go of grasping worldly experience through wisdom is letting go of self-view, based on Buddha's Dhamma. To do that, you need to understand life experience with wisdom.

Ordinary wisdom can help some people develop resilience; noble wisdom can help a person cease suffering in a stable manner.

Evidence based scientific studies have shown that people who experience distressing events, such as job loss, death, or relationship break ups and alike tend to develop hard earned wisdom, and that self-reflection is helpful to developing hard-earned wisdom (Gluck et al., 2019, Weststrate and Gluck, 2017). Try to understand your mind's natural way of working, how it tends to get carried away with delusion when experiencing the world. You may reflect on yourself to reveal the truth about yourself and try to understand the consequences of delusion; for example, you may think that in the past, you regretted or cried a lot when you lost things but crying or regretting didn't bring you anything - only tiredness. If you were to apply wisdom, you would understand that experiencing tiredness is meaningless. This is one way to investigate, reflect on yourself, and apply wisdom to worldly experiences in daily life. This can be practiced by anyone regardless of their conventional background.

Ordinary wisdom helps reduce suffering, and noble wisdom contributes to the cessation of suffering stably across the stages of nibbana. Practicing developing wisdom can prevent unwanted distress for people who choose to release their mind's burden and the struggles that arise from worldly experiences stemming from sensory information. Should you wish to reduce the mind's burden and suffering to experience more peace and happiness, you can develop the noble path step by step while doing everyday things. We can use simple mathematical equation to explain things.

> Understanding sensory information leads to an understanding of sensory information.

> Understanding sensory information and wisdom [12]together enables you to consciously apply wisdom in daily life through deliberate efforts.

> Understanding sensory information through the Sotapanna and the four-fold nibbana = understanding that surpasses the common way of receiving, interpreting and making sense of sensory information.

Standard social life and spiritual life are two different paths. Standard social life, or the way of standard thinking, is that when you get things you like, you become happy, and lose things, you become sad. When expectation does not align with the true experience (e.g., I should have won, I should have gotten that job based on expectation),

[12] Wisdom can be learned through practice, and your conventional background is not relevant.

understand that expectation is a delusion and lower it as much as possible. If you were to try something different; when you don't get a job, lose things, accept them and let them go without touching them in mind again and again. Instead of making worrisome experiences a long-lasting pain, let them go as quickly as possible, if possible, instantly.

If you seek a way out of distress, you may expand on faith. Faith in what?

Faith refers to understanding universal rhythm; ups and downs are part of life. Once you understand the nature, you may apply wisdom to let go of limited vision to self, social practices, and worldly experiences.

To experience Sotapanna, you may not bother too much about body or form as yet. This is because the path is gradual.

Chapter 22
Noble Sangha, the disciples who represent Buddha through shaping karma

One way in which you could understand the appearance of a universal Buddha and Buddhas through the noble Sangha route is that they don't cling to social practices. But sometimes, this can make those who do not know much about Sotapanna or nibbana a bit confused and puzzled. This is because sometimes those who seek Sotapanna or nibbana may not properly understand the aspect of the universal Dhamma that arises from rituals and social practices. Thus, it is beneficial to understand and remind yourself again and again that Sotapanna or nibbana is a happening based on karma or universal laws, not on rituals.

Universal laws impact one's wisdom and many other things, but because an ordinary person cannot necessarily understand karma through sensory information, an average person might not comprehend it unless they develop the upper stages of nibbana, triple knowledge, and beyond.

Typically, Sotapanna is not something one comes to experience in modern day meditation classes or retreats. Instead, it is an unexpected occurrence for someone who has completed merits, shaped by karma, to experience a wholesome state based on wisdom. The only thing you don't get to hear about the Sotapanna experience is due to the rare appearances of the noble Sangha, and also because some of those who run meditation sessions might fear losing income through such things as they value material gains more than they value true Dhamma. The truth is that a person who experiences Sotapanna to Arahansthip typically experiences such mind states at random times shaped by one's own karma.

> "Uggasena, who was still on top of the pole, attained Arahatship."- Dhp 348

When Buddha didn't follow social norms, some who didn't comprehend Buddha's state of mind commented that what Buddha did was not appropriate. Regardless of others' comments, Buddha went beyond social practices.

> "The Buddha Gotama does not bow or respect to old brahmins, elderly and senior, who are advanced in years and have reached the final stage of life; nor does he rise in their presence or offer them a seat." And this is indeed the case, for the worthy Gotama does not bow to old brahmins, elderly and senior, who are advanced in years and have reached the final stage of life; nor does he rise in their presence or offer them a seat. This is not appropriate, worthy Gotama.'

> Then it occurred to me, 'These spiritual friends don't know what a senior is, or what qualities make you a senior.'
>
> Friends, suppose you're eighty, ninety, or a hundred years old. But your speech is untimely, false, meaningless, and against the universal teaching or training. You say things at the wrong time which are worthless, unreasonable, rambling, and unbeneficial to end samsara or mental distress. Then you'll be reckoned a 'childish senior'.
>
> Now suppose you're a youth, young, with pristine black hair, blessed with youth, in the prime of life. But your speech is timely, true, meaningful, and in line with the teaching and training. You say things at the right time which are valuable, reasonable, succinct, and beneficial for others so that they can practice and experience universal dhamma. Then you'll be reckoned an 'astute senior'."- Dutiyauruvelasutta, AN 4.22

Pay close attention here; Buddha's words go beyond social practices, which may appear rebellious without harming anyone. However, if you were to follow social practices with wholehearted giving too much importance to such things, then you are rejecting the teachings of the universal Buddha. Yet when you hear these words, you may want to investigate your thoughts, and check whether you have been rejecting the teachings of the universal Buddha. If you understand that you have rejected Buddha by embracing social practices fully hearted without recognizing that there are things on earth — universal phenomena that shape worldly experiences — you may renew your understanding, transforming it from a previous lack of understanding of universal truths.

The reason why you want to understand the truths that are universally applicable is to experience cessation from distress naturally through wisdom, so that you don't have to put any conscious effort [13]into applying wisdom. You tend to get hungry naturally without having to consciously produce. You tend to feel thirsty naturally without having to artificially make you thirsty. In the same way, nibbana or Sotapanna makes you not experience distress naturally without having to produce conscious effects.

> "All Buddhas, whether in the past, the Buddhas of the future, and the Buddha at present—destroyer of the sorrows of many—respecting the universally applicable dhamma and practice or true teaching they did live, they do live, and they also will live. This is the nature of the Buddhas.
>
> Therefore, someone who desires self-knowledge of freedom from mental distress coming from worldly experience due to delusion, and aspires to experience nibbana themselves, should respect the universal

---

[13] It's comfortable and natural, unlike when you have to put in effort to apply wisdom and struggle to do so. That particular moment you experience Sotapanna completely transforms your mind state, so that the kinds of sorrows and miseries a person experiences in an ordinary mind state naturally disappear. These days, there are certain therapies that aim to teach you how to let go of distress through conscious efforts, and the need for such therapies disappears as you experience Sotapanna.

> dhamma or true teaching, remembering the instructions of the Buddhas."- Paṭhamauruvelasutta, AN 4.21

Life seems like a living movie: experiences keep coming and going, and it feels true but not stable. Thus, one has to be careful in understanding about what appears to be the truth. When you stop mistaking untruths for truth, that's when you understand the truth.

> "It's not the earth property that makes the true Dhamma disappear. It's not the water property the fire property the wind property that makes the true Dhamma disappear. It's growth in lack of wisdom and wrong view among spiritual friends and community of sangha who make the universal Dhamma disappear."
> - Saddhammapatirupaka Sutta, SN 16.13

The truth about oneself goes beyond what a person thinks of themselves based on conventions and social practices. The truths about social practices lie beyond what you think of its value. The true version of the Triple Gem that an ordinary person and trainees[14] need to associate with in order to experience nibbana or Sotapanna lies beyond what appears to be the Triple Gem.

If there are special trainings for spiritual friends in monasteries that differ from those for spiritual friends in homes, or vice versa, that is revealing a social path. What is common

[14] Trainees refer to Sotapannas, Sakadagamis, and Anagamis.

to all is the universal training path. Over time, due to the dispersion of the universal Sangha and merely through carrying Dhamma by ordinary Sangha and sharing what was heard and not what they know over centuries, the ways in which you can link the conventional path to the universal path and the correct interpretation of Dhamma have been lost. This has led to a misinterpretation of the universal Dhamma, preventing right view, the noble path, and practice for those who seek them. There are many conventional paths, but there is one universal path. All conventional paths meet at the entry of the universal path.

You may follow whatever conventional path or the basics; nowadays, there are many divisions of conventional Dhamma and conventional sangha, but regardless, there is one noble path for all. Perhaps you did not know or thought of it but all those who claim they follow Dhamma or are seeking universal truth are part of the same community, each contributing in different ways. For example, many great Arahants represented and contributed to the nibbana in the past. Then, with the decline in the number of Arahants over the centuries, many ordinary Sanghas who have good faith have contributed conventional Dhamma across the world; they shared the basics or conventionally limited Dhamma. Then, there are those who explain how you can go link conventional Dhamma to universal Dhamma, and those who reveal Sotapanna to Arahant—they share the higher Dhamma in contemporary context. In this manner, all the Sanghas together contribute to revealing the universal Dhamma within their capacity. Thus, you must not think that when someone experiences four stages of nibbana as someone who is not a friend of yours; rather, you should treat them as the best friend you have, for the purpose of revealing how you can escape your mental distress with wisdom in a stable manner.

It's not that those who become Sotapanna to Arahant invent or discover a new version of Dhamma, rather they reveal precisely what was revealed by the universal Buddha. If you want to understand universal truth, what has been revealed to human beings by the universal Buddha, you may develop three qualities within you: give up blind faith, meaning just don't think anyone who wears a monastic dress (or non-monastic dress) preaches the correct Dhamma instead listen and hear when Dhamma-related matters are shared, examine what they say, investigate and question Dhamma-related matters, if you have doubts, approach those who claim they know about nibbana for themselves and apply wisdom to clarify doubts. A person can give something to you only when they have something, and what Arahants have for them is only renunciation —letting go of grasping fetters. Worldly experiences don't have empathy for anyone. Gone beyond worldly experiences and gone beyond divisions or conventions, they don't divide people based on conventions, and thus, they can offer you an insight, right view from which the noble path begins. This truth is revealed to spiritual friends who seek the universal noble path with immense loving kindness.

> "And how does a person who has noble friends as friends, companions, & comrades, develop & pursue the noble eightfold path? There is the case where a person develops right view."- Upaddha Sutta, SN 45.2

To experience Sotapanna state, you may include multiple components; you may be committed to understanding yourself, letting go of grasping the self and social practices to begin with while developing noble virtues. To develop noble virtues, you may develop beyond precepts and monastic rules; try to maintain noble precepts, which means include refraining from false and harmful speech (bear in mind, wrong view of Dhamma is harmful as it can prevent nibbana), refrain from backbiting, refrain from using harsh and abusive language with an intent to harm or hurt another, refrain from engaging in meaningless conversations or avoid talking things that are not relevant for experiencing nibbana or Sotapanna, and avoid wrong means of livelihood into whatever the kind of precepts and monastic rules you are undertaking now, while developing the right view. In the meantime, try to better understand the universally applicable Triple Gem. Understanding of the universally applicable Triple Gem is an understanding of a Sotapanna.

Chapter 23
The core of Dhamma

What Buddha taught was how you can experience the four stages of nibbana, and not that you merely engage in practices that don't produce the blissful Sotapanna state in mind. The reason for the lack of fruition is that the core has not been developed. When the core is missing, the surface alone cannot reduce the distress. Thus, understand how to reduce mental stress in daily life by understanding the core. Due to the decline of Buddha's Dhamma, spiritual friends often mix things up. To avoid mixed-up practices and to know the direct practices, it's useful for you to understand what the Triple Gem is when you intend to commence the noble path.

1. What is universal Buddha?

   Buddhhood is a state of wisdom beyond conventional understanding of self, social practices and other fetters.
2. What is nibbana or Sotapanna?

   Universal Dhamma is a transformation in a mental continuum, it is a happening like birth.
3. What is universal Sangha?

   Whoever has let go of the deluded understanding of the fetters in mind, regardless of external factors.

Buddha's Dhamma has been misrepresented for over a thousand years. Misinterpretations have led to the loss of the noble view and the noble path. What Buddha has predicted has been happening over centuries. Why do we need to discuss this? Because it is by following the path precisely as explained by the Buddha that one can experience nibbana or Sotapanna, and otherwise, cannot. Just by following secondary practices, or things that are not directly contributing to experiencing the Dhamma, one cannot experience Sotapanna. Thus, it is important for you to know precisely what to train and how to train the mind. Sotapanna teaches you to awaken the mind to wisdom. That is to let go of the mental distress you fabricate and experience for yourself. For example, when the mind makes up competition, strives for pride, develops greed, and hatred, fires tend to arise, and experience within, and Sotapanna makes it possible to be free from such things in the mind naturally. To experience such a state, you may apply wisdom to let go of grasping the self and worldly experiences.

Nibbana is an understanding. A child's understanding differs from that of an adult. A scientist's understanding differs from that of a school child. A pet's understanding differs from that of its caretaker or owner. A blind man's understanding differs from that of someone with good vision. Understanding differs among people. Understanding changes over time, depending on context and experiences that arise based on sensory information. Surpassing ordinary understanding with wisdom is the path to Sotapanna, and it involves understanding beyond the conventional self, rituals, social practices, and the universally applicable Triple Gem to let go of doubts.

By understanding conventional self with wisdom, you can at least reduce the mental distress arising from your daily life until you attain Sotapanna. To overcome self-view or distress stemming from self, you may apply wisdom with patience. Rituals and social practices encourage you to get things in a hurry, hurry to get a job, hurry to gain something, and so on. Instead, in spiritual life, you may develop patience to experience whatever it is, and let go of delusion. Let's say you lost a job. Instead of getting overly sad, understand that even if you gain everything now, it won't last forever or remain stable, so making yourself restless and distressed over changing worldly experiences is not wise. Doing things you can do to resolve issues without getting too anxious or restless is wise.

Rituals and social practices encourage you to divide life experience as good and bad and so on. Social practices encourage you to refuse certain experiences, such as illnesses and losses. Instead, to follow the noble path that is universally applicable, you may develop wisdom to awaken to true life experiences; illnesses, death, ups, and downs are part of life.

Rituals and social practices encourage you to gain things, gain materials, respect, and like. Rituals and social practices encourage you to gain things, gain materials, respect, and like. The spiritual life shows you how to give up giving too much importance to material things, relationships, and worldly experiences, as they are subject to change, and what changes can cause distress.

To experience the best of worldly experiences, you may cut off the root cause of suffering or delusion. You may apply wisdom to cut off delusion in daily life. Practicing the noble path requires you to apply wisdom to letting go of distress stemming from worldly experiences. Depending on context, for example, you may let go of getting distress; "I didn't get that job but it's ok, I don't regret it", "I didn't win but I wouldn't worry about it, or "My associates are unhappy, that's ok as long as I know I've done good in line with noble Dhamma" and likewise. In this way, social life or conventions and spiritual life are two different ways, and to experience nibbana or Sotapanna, you just have to understand spiritual life while living your social life.

Nibbana or Sotapanna is about letting go of deluded understanding of self and worldly experiences, an understanding with wisdom.

> "... Ignorance is the origin of choices. When ignorance ceases, choices cease.

> The practice that leads to the cessation of choices is simply this noble eightfold path, that is: right view..." - Bhikkhusutta, SN 12.28

Typically, when the path to Sotapanna or higher Dhamma is shared, we invite those who feel that the words of higher Dhamma are for them, and why? First, because those who have completed ten paramis in previous lives will tend to have their hearts call them to hear higher Dhamma, even if they don't know it for now, as it evolves. This explains why Buddha visited those who had the potential to experience nibbana, not just everyone. There are some spiritual practitioners who can experience nibbana now; this is not to discourage others, but others may develop over time in samsara. Depending on how you strengthen your practice, aligning with the noble way of practicing, you will get to renounce distress coming from worldly experience with stability across stages of nibbana.

Second, for ethical reasons, beings should be free to make their choices and do what they like. Just because a person makes a choice that is different from another, that should not be a reason to dislike anyone at a personal level. This is how you should understand noble aspects related to nibbana. To develop the noble view, you may understand that a bhikkhu is a mind state, not external factors.

Arising, continuing and passing is a way of universal rhythm. You are a part of the universe, and the universe is within you. You consume food, drink fluids, and breathe oxygen repeatedly, which are then transformed into various forms such as energy in your body and mind, bodily fluids, and carbon dioxide and the like. These substances then re-enter the universe, and you consume things from the universe and vice versa. Among the things that happen between you and the universe, there are two kinds of things: there are things you can see and hear, and there are things you cannot see or hear and the like. For example, you can't see your own face from your eyes without a mirror. You can see your thoughts as they appear on a separate screen and understand them with wisdom naturally, when you experience the four stages of nibbana.

Some of your thoughts can disappear immediately after they occur; some of your family of thoughts can last for a day, a week, a month, a year, ten years, twenty years, or even fifty years. Some family of thoughts can sustain as fuel that has the potential to generate a new life after the death of the physical body. Nibbana cut of the fuel or family of thoughts that has the potential to generate a new life across stages, something you can't see for yourself unless developed the triple knowledge and beyond. You may initially understand the lower stages of Dhamma.

Chapter 24
Barriers to developing the universal noble path

There are many barriers to developing the universal noble path. One of which is the lack of understanding of the noble path and its practice. Here, we discuss some of these barriers and suggest practices to overcome them.

First, most people attempt to acquire knowledge about nibbana or Sotapanna from ancient writings. If you were to follow Dhamma merely through ancient writings, chances are you will be unlikely to experience nibbana or Sotapanna. This is because, to a greater extent, such books don't specify the techniques for training your mind or the direct practices. Instead, they present brief information that isn't sufficient to understand how to train the mind to become a Sotapanna. In addition, ancient writings were conveyed solely through oral transmission, based on what people heard or assumed about nibbana, rather than what they knew. Thus, the books summarize certain things without revealing in-depth practice with accuracy and interpretation needing enhancement. Knowing what's in the book and memorising it alone is the basic thing. Thereafter, one needs to apply what's been said in practice. If you happen to merely memorise what's in books but don't apply to yourself, you can't experience nibbana or Sotapanna. During Buddha's time, people had no books, but they experienced nibbana or Sotapanna.

Second, if you were to follow common meditation practices of modern days, such as concentrating on breath, objects, sensations, and similar practices, chances are you will not experience nibbana or Sotapanna because the practice of Sotapanna is maintaining the right view during waking hours. It's not mere concentration but applying wisdom to understand self and beyond within usual activities.

Third, inability to understand matters related to self and the universe can act as a barrier to the path. Given that Dhamma and Sangha are matters related to universal laws or karma, not rituals, it would be of benefit if you avoid measuring external factors. Instead, those who seek the true version of Buddha's Dhamma may measure someone's understanding of the four stages of nibbana. That is because nibbana or Sotapanna is an understanding of self, worldly experiences, and fetters, regardless of external factors. Then, if you were to question, why have we told that monks are ritually made for a thousand years? The answer is that, due to the scarcity and decline of universal Dhamma, over the years, what's left has been rituals, and people only know about such things these days because they haven't heard about universal Dhamma and universal Sangha for a long time. Truth is rare, and although it is rare, what you need to understand is that, in any case, Buddha did not say that rituals lead to nibbana or Sotapanna; rather, karma leads to experiencing four stages of nibbana.

There is a correlation between wisdom and karma. A being experiences human form, noble wisdom, and many other things by shaping universal laws including karma and developing the mirror of Buddha, Dhamma, and Sangha within.

> "Friends don't be afraid to do deeds of merit. This is a synonym for happiness that is desirable, pleasing, charming, dear, and agreeable, that is 'meritorious deeds…"- Itv 22, Māpuññabhāyi Sutta

> "One whose confirmed confidence in the Tathāgata is well-established, unshakable in mind having experienced fourfold nibbana; who has noble virtues, who has confirmed confidence in the noble Saṅgha, & has the noble view: not poor, they say of him. Not in vain his life…"- AN 4.52, Puññābhisanda Sutta

Uncovering the noble path involves addressing the root cause of suffering and applying wisdom to daily life. Wisdom is when you are sad, upset, anxious and alike, understanding that sadness and the like is a part of life, and how to make the best out of the sadness experience. For example, when you face a problem, try not to be too sad; instead, focus more attention on resolving the problem. It's a more helpful approach to life because, when you are too sad, you struggle to find the energy to deal with the issue or resolve things. This is how you get to know about yourself better and renounce worldly experiences. Having some faith and wisdom can be helpful in making your progress, but what exactly is it that you have faith in? If you have a faith that the self and your worldly experiences are empty of a permanent self, that is your faith. If you believe that you experience mental distress through worldly experiences in daily life, that is your preliminary stage of awakening (before Sotapanna) to true life experience. You may practice reducing your deluded understanding of self and social practices from the outset, along with doubts about sufferings within daily life, while connecting with a spiritual friend who is a representative of the universal Triple Gem.

Honouring and appreciating the universal Triple Gem remains beneficial for those seeking to train for Buddhahood, a state of wisdom. This is because when you respect and appreciate something, it grows within you and helps purify your delusions. However, you can't pick and choose or create a representation of the universal Triple Gem through man-made choices, as these choices alone cannot escape samsara or the process of universal functioning.

Although universal laws, rhythm, and order remain largely unknown to ordinary people, there is an order in the universe. Universal order is empty of the delusion of the mental fetters.

A small stream of water, when joined with a larger body of water such as an ocean, expands. In the same way, a mind that has impurity can grow in purity by connecting with the larger sources of purity in line with universal order and rules. This led to the teacher of Gods and humans, one who knows the universe better than any other human beings, the universal Buddha, to explain how you should provide[15] and respect, considering the fruition not because Buddha wanted gains and honour for himself, but because they allow others to experience Buddhahood though nature's way and universal functioning. Yet over time, some of the ordinary people among the Sangha wanted to hide the truth from you so they could receive benefits and make a living out of Dhamma; merely eat, sleep, and run a few retreats or classes without having to put in the hard work to purify within themselves. At the same time, among the ordinary Sangha are those who are truly committed to Buddha and Dhamma. They have tried their best to preserve what's left; a snapshot of information about nibbana written in ancient books has been carried over thousands of years, and it is a matter of understanding beyond what's in the ancient books that will aid you to train the mind to experience Sotapanna.

Given the lifespan is short, you may strive with urgency to practice something different from what you've practiced before. Thus, by now, you should know that what you have been doing

[15] Dana, or providing materials, skills, your time, etc.

is not the practice recommended for the noble path. Instead, you may consider changing your practices. For example, you may offer support and honour for the ordinary Sangha for helping them to develop the right view. You may offer support and respect to your family and friends as needs arise within your capacity. You may offer support and honour to the universal Sangha for helping you understand the universal Dhamma. In this way, you may help yourself and others without hurting anyone, within your capacity and with good intentions.

When you come to seek universal truths or Buddha's path, always remind yourself that you have not come to practice it merely to find a way to survive; eat food, find accommodation, and show off to the world, but something more precious than such things, and that is to end suffering with stability while also surviving, eating, sleeping and doing usual things.

Once you are born, you understand yourself as "you". Even young infants have an underlying tendency for greed and hate. Nibbana cuts off the underlying tendency for delusion, greed, and hate naturally across stages. Developing noble wisdom requires you to let go of the delusion of the self. To let go of delusion, you may adopt certain techniques. For example, understand that good and bad are part of life and try not to divide experiences into good and bad. Try to maintain this understanding throughout the day and night. Try lowering expectations by understanding that not all expectations can be fulfilled; sometimes they will, and other times they will not, and so on. Take responsibility for your own intentional actions. Avoid comparing yourself to others with the intent to downgrade others as people. Help everyone in any way you can. Avoid giving too much value to social practices or don't make a big deal out of conventions, as they are temporary.

You may fulfill your responsibilities to others. As you do, you may maintain the understanding that others may not always appreciate your efforts. By understanding this, you may reduce expectations of any appreciation. Avoid lying, misinterpreting, or pretending to know everything about nibbana until you have experienced it for yourself. You may avoid seeking special treatment for yourself. Maintain loving-kindness for all beings in every thought. This means treating everyone with care and avoiding differential treatment based on rituals, social practices and conventions. Bear in mind that Arahants treat everyone with respect; for some of you, it's just that you can't imagine how that would be. If you want to let go of the self-view that bothers you, develop similar qualities. Use things for their intended purposes without misusing or grasping at them. Understand that if you were to actually practice aspects related to nibbana or Sotapanna in this manner, not mere rituals, you will enhance your chances to let go of mental distress in daily life with stability and experience blissful fourfold nibbana.

Chapter 25
Let go of the lack of wisdom

One way in which you can renounce worldly life in the universal noble path is understanding that every time you take something as "pleasurable", or "happy" and likewise in the world, as it changes, they always carry the possibility of turning into displeasures. Things you see as one thing come as two things, meaning youth becomes old, birth brings death, and likewise. You may see one thing, not necessarily see the second things that come with it. Thus, awaken your mind with wisdom to understand beyond what you experience at each moment.

Sometimes, what you expect will happen, and other times it will not. Thus, if you expect everything you desire to occur consistently, that is a delusion. Instead, awaken yourself to let go of that delusion. When you take action, sometimes things will go right, and sometimes they will go wrong. Understand the truths applicable in life as a truth seeker. You may think of alternatives: if this happens, I will do this way; if it does not happen, I will do that way and likewise. Truth is truth, and while some people may not like hearing it, wise individuals within the ordinary sangha typically seek to understand the truth, whether it is pleasant or unpleasant or regardless of such labels and conventions. It is for their benefit, truth is shared.

Untrue things, meaning things that are not stable, may seem pleasant on the surface. A conventional lifestyle, whether in a monastery or at home, may initially seem familiar, pleasant on the surface, and easy to understand, as things are already established, and you've known such things for a long time. On the other hand, the noble path may seem unknown, and thus, you may discover it. Many face one of the biggest barriers: the tendency to follow only what's known and pleasant on the surface. They do not discover something new and more blissful than they've known since birth. Yet to discover, one must seek, ask questions wisely, and investigate. Few investigate with wisdom. Many blindly follow whatever is told to them. If you seek truth, adopt a mode of discovery. Buddha's path is closed to those who do not. This is true whether a person lives at home or in a monastic setting. Setting is not the issue. Mind and wisdom are.

The noble path may seem initially unpleasant as untrained mind can struggle to reduce likes or dislikes or expectations from worldly experiences grounded in delusion. Then you may remind yourself that what you've known so far since birth are worldly pleasures. As you discover noble path, you will come to know pleasures beyond worldly pleasures; some things are left for you to discover. You may awaken your wisdom to see beyond your conventional lifestyles. Therefore, whether you're enjoying moments with your family, working, or living a monastic lifestyle, to make the most of your experience; you can fulfill your responsibilities while appreciating various aspects of your life or the company of your associates or friends, family, and children or living in the places you prefer. In doing so, you enhance your mind state. However, take extra time to remind yourself to reflect on the fact that your worldly experience is not stable, and that changes are a natural part of life. When you evaluate the instability of self and worldly experiences to a reasonable standard, you should find that you have reduced deluded understanding of self and the world, meaning you have reduced excessive expectations regarding worldly experiences in your mind and ability to experience the best of each moment. By doing so, you can flourish in both your conventional life and your spiritual life.

When seeking universal Dhamma, try not to overly depend on rituals, as a Sotapanna is a happening based on universal laws of karma. During the time of Buddha, individuals who attained the stages of Sotapanna, Sakadagami, Anagami, and Arahant were able to publicly declare their status and accept donations intended for ordinary people seeking to cultivate wisdom and merit, regardless of their appearance or conventional background. Over the years, this understanding became distorted, and the term "monk" began to be associated primarily with those who followed specific rituals. When Buddha intended one meaning, but the ordinary Sangha interprets it differently in contemporary times, the correct understanding is hindered, leading to wrong views that diverge from the Dhamma. For example, in the noble path, Sotapannas and Sakadagamis are considered householders because they still retain the fetter of sensuality (or indulge in sensual pleasures). Anagamis and Arahants serve as monks who have given up lower fetters based of noble understanding. Those who have not experienced at least the state of Sotapanna are considered outsiders. Keep a steady goal, stay focused, and strengthen your practice to let go of fetters to experience Sotapanna.

> "...Then if one wants one may state about oneself: 'Hell is ended; animal wombs are ended; the state of the hungry shades is ended; states of deprivation, destitution, the bad bourns are ended! I am a stream-winner, steadfast, never again destined for states of woe, headed for self-awakening!..."- Gihi Sutta, AN 5.179

> "Nandiya, someone who totally and utterly lacks these four factors of stream-entry is an outsider who belongs with the ordinary persons, I say."- Nandiyasakkasutta, SN 55.40

Spiritual friends in monasteries and homes who want to represent universal Buddha and universal Dhamma may develop the right understanding of nibbana and share with their followers. Understand that it is not impossible but possible for you to experience the Sotapanna if you adopt the noble practice based on right view grounded on wisdom.

Chapter 26
Turning universal waves

Concerning the practice leading to the noble path and first fetters, which include self-view, conventions, and social practices, we can discuss this in more detail. Understand universal ways of functioning: worldly pleasures coming from sensory experiences do not come alone; they always carry the possibility of turning into displeasures as they change. When the universe brings changes and your sensory information shifts, and as your worldly experiences change, view it as an opportunity to awaken yourself to universal truths. What applies universally is that worldly experiences are constantly changing. Sometimes, what you expect will happen, and other times it will not. Thus, if you expect everything you desire to occur consistently, that is a delusion. Instead, awaken yourself to let go of that delusion.

Change is a fundamental aspect of life; you are part of the universe, and the universal functioning experienced within each person are fluid, not stable. Therefore, instead of grasping onto socially created concepts of self and the world, seek wisdom to let go of mental pain. When you hear about the universal noble path, you may hear things beyond what you commonly heard. As you continue training your mind to let go of delusion, you will experience things you have not experienced before. Eat well, dress well, live well, and take care of yourself. Fulfil your responsibilities to others and make the best of both your worldly life and your spiritual life as they come as a twin package for a Sotapanna (a stream-enterer).

> "A Sotapanna who grows in ten ways grows nobly, taking on what is essential and excellent in this life by giving up what is unwise. What ten? One grows materialistically (in fields and lands, money and grain, associates (families or friends, supporters, workers, and staff, and in livestock). And one grows in spiritual life (confirmed confidence in the universal Triple Gem, noble ethics, in-depth understanding of self and conventions, generosity, and noble wisdom."- Vaḍḍhisutta, AN 10.74

To experience the best of life, you may awaken wisdom to experience Sotapanna.

Chapter 27
Primary Dhamma practices

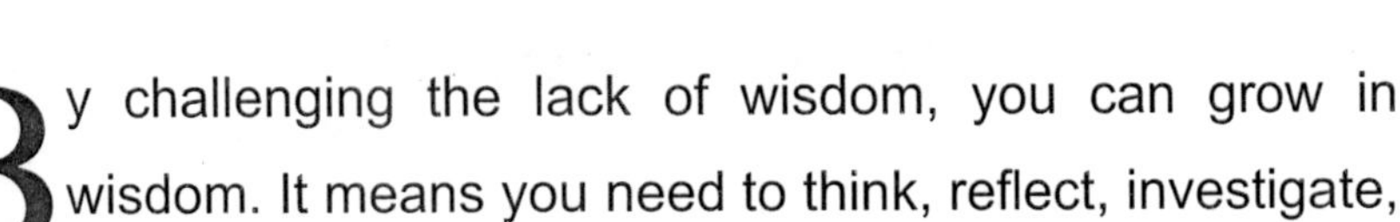

By challenging the lack of wisdom, you can grow in wisdom. It means you need to think, reflect, investigate, and find the answer in a reasonable manner to let go of wisdom.

If you focus primarily on developing secondary practices (i.e. rituals, conventional lifestyles, precepts or monastic rules without developing wisdom based path to Sotapanna), you may not attain nibbana. The majority of spiritual practitioners do not experience nibbana or Sotapanna because they do not practice what is truly important and instead engage in activities that do not significantly contribute to the noble Path. However, if you prioritize the development of primary Dhamma practices that are directly related to experiencing Sotapanna, regardless of your secondary practices, you will be in a better position to achieve Sotapanna and beyond. So, what are these primary practices? They involve investigating the mind, understanding your thoughts, and examining how they grasp self or social practices, as well as any doubts you may have about life experiences. If you happen to have doubts regarding suffering, meaning that you think your life experiences are satisfying, you are unlikely to want to give up grasping life experiences. On the other hand, if you happen to think your life experience is suffering because you have had certain bad events[16] that caused you distress in life, you are more likely to give up grasping worldly experiences that cause you pain. When you realize that certain life experiences cause suffering, you are more likely to seek ways to reduce stress, enhance peace and happiness, and improve the quality of your mind and life. When you feel like you've had enough of distress through worldly experiences, suffering is horrible and unworthy to continue, you are more likely to find a way out. If you happen to think suffering is unworthy, and peace is precious, you tend to hold onto what you consider precious. If you consider that a moment of peace and happiness is precious, that will aid you in applying wisdom beyond what you experience through sensory information to let go of distress and to develop the noble path. When you understand from your own experience that worrying over certain things won't necessarily change anything but will only make you weary and meaningless, you will find it easy to let go of worrying over worrying things. In this manner, the universally applicable noble path requires you to understand your life experience with wisdom in mind.

---

[16] Bad events are personal experiences in which an ordinary person feels deeply hurt, regardless of how they are seen by a third party or an outsider.

You may also address doubts you have regarding the universal Buddha, and address doubts regarding universal Dhamma. For example, you might experience thoughts about whether the Triple Gem and universal laws are real, or not, or whether nibbana transforms how you experience the world, or not, and so on. To address doubts, you require investigating and testing subject matters or Dhamma matters with wisdom. Through Dhamma, you can see both the universal Buddha and the universal Sanghas. Questing is vital and applying wisdom too. This brings us to the question: How can you let go of grasping or attachment? You can release grasping or attachment by opening your mind to wisdom. When you investigate your mind, you may see both your strengths and weaknesses. Recognizing your weaknesses can help you understand that when your mind is attached. You may investigate your thoughts that produce distress. For example, if you feel upset or anxious, question yourself: "Why do I feel anxious?" The likely answer might be that you expect too much from worldly experiences based on sensory information. By understanding both what you expect and what can happen, you can approach life with greater wisdom. The mind can become quite unsettled when influenced by delusion. To lessen this shakiness and bring balance, apply wisdom in your daily life as much as possible through conscious efforts. To enhance your conscious efforts and facilitate personal growth, you may consider connecting with noble friends. A barrier faced by those seeking stable peace or Sotapanna these days is that most do not understand who the noble Sanghas are. The decline of true Dhamma since Buddha's parinirvana over a thousand years ago has, in general, led people to no longer understand the universal Sanghas. To understand noble Sanghas, you may investigate subject matters: how someone explains Dhamma, whether they explain it as a universal happening out of rituals, and their ability to explain the direct practices, precise information regarding the four-fold nibbana. Nibbana is an understanding. Whoever understands direct practices and is able to explain words of Dhamma precisely as explained by the Buddha, beyond rituals and social practices, is likely to represent the true version of the Sanghas or the universal Sangha.

A person may respect someone wearing monastic dress as a noble one and continue to develop wrong views while ignoring someone who is a Sotapannna wearing poor clothing. Yet, given that nibbana or Sotapanna relates to universal truths and the universe knows, taking the untrue as true makes one unable to develop mirror-like Dhamma within. Not understanding the noble Sangha, chances are you are likely to go with samsara. You may awaken to see the universal truths; karma-based Dhamma and karma-based Sangha.

> "Suppabuddha, the leper, while sitting at the back of the crowd and listening attentively to the discourse

> given by the Buddha, attained Sotapatti Fruition. When the crowd had dispersed, he followed the Buddha to the monastery as he wished to tell the Buddha about his attainment of Sotapatti Fruition."- Dhp 66

The path to the cessation of distress requires one to understand the universe within. The world is created within. When you see stars in the sky, people, forests, and roads, it's not that you actually see them; rather, a mirror image of such things is created within, and the world and the universe are experienced there. In the same way, it's not that you get to see Buddha, Dhamma, and Sangha outside, but the mental image of the Triple Gem is created within. The true version of the Triple Gem cannot be understood or seen as a mirror image within you unless you let go of the first three fetters while taking refuge in the universal Triple Gem in your mental continuum. By letting go of three fetters, when a person experiences a mirror image of Buddha and Dhamma within them, their mind-body is the temple or monastery itself, not an external building. If someone were to ignore Buddha's disciples who carry Buddha and Dhamma within their mind-body through shaping karma, they would put themselves in a position where they are unable to connect with the universally applicable Triple Gem and, as a consequence, unable to extinguish the fires within. In other words, a person can take an untrue version of the Triple Gem as true because they carry delusion within or grasp self-view, rituals, and social practices. As long as a person continues not to purify themselves from delusion to self and social practices within, while taking refuge in the true version of the Triple Gem, they are bound to continue in samsara, as they continue to generate fuel within while touching the universe and worldly experience.

As we are talking about matters related to the universe and universal laws, or karma, it should be noted that when someone lets go of delusion for self-view and other-fetters by taking refuge in the universal Triple Gem, their path to universal Dhamma opens up. Given that the universal Buddha's purifying energies are immense and remain in the universe for many years to come, a person becomes a disciple of the Buddha by experiencing the mirror image[17] of the Buddha and nibbana across stages within as they experience lower and upper stages of universal Dhamma; that's when they are been invited, come bhikku or "ehi Bhikku", as they experience the last stage of nibbana from the Buddha in line with universal laws.

---

[17] Human beings have sensors that can interpret patterns in light, sound, nerve impulses, etc. But you are seeing light, not the object itself. Plus, those sensors are translating everything into electricity in the brain. That's two whole layers of abstraction. Most of what we've built is based on similar waves and foundations. Thus, everything you see is like a mirror image, a part of the mind's way of understanding the world.

Chapter 28
Treat as the most precious

A person experiences the world and the universe within. Given that the universe is within you, it knows all about you and produces consequences in line with what's within and the universal laws.

The universally applicable nibbana or Sotapanna is the path available to many for escaping suffering, making it precious. When you take something as precious, that means you truly value it. When you value something, you tend to grow on it. Developing Dhamma is about letting go of illusions about the self and, social practices, while contemplating the Triple Gem.

When someone values universal Dhamma in their heart, they are inclined to develop Dhamma within. Dhamma is not a mere ritual, but the extent to which you let go of delusion to self-view; likes, dislikes, expectations, pride, ill will, need to compare one another as people, and the like. In addition, Dhamma is about letting go of delusions to rituals and social practices, so you don't give too much value to rituals or social practices that divide people, instead, you let go of them by applying wisdom. For example, standard ways of doing things and social practices make it a norm to become sad when losing things and become happy when gaining things. Similarly, it seems that society can sometimes portray that one can have a perfect life, perfect relationship, perfect household, perfect school grades, and a perfect job and similar ways. Yet, in real life, it is not always possible to have perfect things, and this is something one gets to learn from one's own life experience, a realization. When the real-life experiences fail to meet what one expects to experience in one's mind, one can feel disappointed. Therefore, by understanding that grasping earthly things too much can bring stress to oneself, you may develop to understand beyond earthly experiences including social practices and rituals.

As you seek truths, you are seeking those related to self, social practices, and the Triple Gem. To discover truths, one needs to ensure false understandings are removed. Thus, if you were to think you are stable, now you need to transform from a falsified understanding to understanding the true-life experience with wisdom. If you were to think of conventional Dhamma as Buddha's Dhamma, now that you need to keep it aside to transform your understanding into something bigger, universal Dhamma across stages. If you had an underlying tendency to think of Sangha as made up of rituals, now that needs to be set aside to transform your understanding to a universal level, and to understand that Sangha is made on universal laws.

Dhamma is primarily a self-practice. You apply Dhamma in your thoughts and become aware of yourself as someone without excessive likes, dislikes, or ill will based on delusion. Dhamma is not merely a ritual. When you do not treat Dhamma as truly precious, you cannot develop wholesome qualities within. Dhamma means not hurting oneself or others. To do this, you may let go of delusion for self and for social practices, at least at the beginning, within your mental continuum. When you know your mental continuum is pure, the universe knows it as pure. In turn, when the universe knows your mental continuum as pure, you know your mental continuum is pure. Therefore, it is beneficial to avoid treating Dhamma as less precious or less valuable than you value the self. This can be explained as follows. For example, if you value gains for yourself, you will seek gains through any means. Instead, if you value Dhamma, chances are you will seek gains merely by a livelihood in line with Dhamma. You can practice non-dhamma through monastic living when you make a living by sharing wrong views or maintain thoughts of delusion. You can practice non-dhamma through household living when you make a living through wrong means.

Dhamma is not outside but your intention. What typically happens is that whoever treats Dhamma as precious and considers Buddha as precious, and vice versa, tends to strictly follow Dhamma even when they have an ordinary mind state.

In this manner, when you value Buddha and Dhamma and those who clarify matters related to Buddha and Dhamma beyond rituals, you will find it easier to develop wholesome Dhamma within. At the beginning, one takes refuge in the Triple Gem to develop it within across stages of Dhamma. At the end, you find refuge within.

You may reflect on the teacher of perfect Dhamma, the universal Buddha, and perfect Dhamma often during the day and night. It will become possible only if you feel like they are worth giving the highest priority for letting go of the distress in your heart. Heartfelt practices can help you develop the universal noble path.

"Friends, when one thing is developed and cultivated, it leads exclusively to disenchantment, dispassion, cessation, peace, insight, enlightenment, and Nibbana. What one thing? Recollection of the Buddha. This one thing, when developed and cultivated, leads exclusively to four-fold nibbana, cessation, peace, insight, enlightenment, and Sotapanna."- AN 1.296

"Monks, when one thing is developed and cultivated, it leads exclusively to disenchantment, dispassion, cessation, peace, insight, enlightenment, and Nibbana. What one thing? Recollection of the noble Dhamma ... Recollection of the noble Saṅgha."- AN 1.297–298

Reflecting on universal Buddha and universal Dhamma during usual activities will aid you in maintaining and developing wholesome within. When someone does not truly value universal Buddha and universal Dhamma within, even if they engage in rituals, they tend not to grow in Dhamma. If you were to truly feel like giving priority to the most precious and the supreme Buddha, you may avoid falsifying the universal Dhamma and develop Dhamma within. If you develop these qualities, it will help you follow the universally applicable noble path. When someone tries to explain the training path to nibbana or Sotapanna without having personally experienced such a state, they can misinterpret the path. This can activate demerits and prevent universal Dhamma. Thus, spiritual friends in monasteries and homes, when they share Dhamma in public, may take extra care when introducing the basics, which will benefit them. For example, one could say, "I heard nibbana has four stages, and this may be the way to experience it, but I am not sure" and alike without falsifying the path. Strive to understand the noble right view first and share the view with those who seek it in the right way.

Remember to constantly practice letting go of "self-view" by means of reducing delusion based likes, dislikes, and expectations while contributing to the well-being of yourself and others in any way you can. Remember it will take time for you to develop your mind to reach such a state, so have patience and continually strive to develop noble wisdom and noble qualities and reach Sotapanna. For example, if you lose something you valued most, learn from it with wisdom to understand that it is normal to lose what you like in life. Try not to dwell on the loss or magnify its impact in your mind. In this manner, when you stop amplifying things about yourself and others and the world, you can retain your ability to remain unaffected by external circumstances by applying wisdom. You may develop a commitment to increase your wisdom.

Chapter 29
Directly related to experiencing the Sotapanna

When you don't engage in practices that are directly related to the Sotapanna, it can be an obstacle to developing stable peace or the four stages of nibbana. Just as the universe within you makes it possible for you to experience the world, the universe also makes it possible to experience cessation from the world, or emptiness within you. The only thing one has to follow is the precise training and develop the mirror of Dhamma within you.

When scientists discover things about the universe, or even about a light bulb or similar things, they can share with others. When they share, others can understand and each person gains understanding through universal energies, as people are connected to each other in some way in line with universal rhythm and laws. In the same way, when nibbana is experienced and shared, others can comprehend and experience because the universal energies allow transmission; the only thing you need to learn is how to get connected in the right way. This brings us to discuss the practice that is directly related to experiencing Sotapanna.

What are the practices that are directly related to experiencing Sotapanna?

Letting go of the first three fetters.

How to let go of the first three fetters?

By understanding beyond self-view and rituals with wisdom, and by understanding the universally applicable Triple Gem.

Understand where you can go wrong when you come to follow the universally applicable spiritual path. Instead of letting go of delusion to self-view, if someone develops more and more self-view; greediness, ill will, expectations, and the like, even if they were to follow rituals or today's meditation practices, the Sotapanna state cannot be experienced. Meditation in the noble path refers to maintaining the right view during waking hours. Moreover, if someone gives social practices undue importance out of delusion, Sotapanna cannot be experienced. This is because one misunderstands social practices as the path to Sotapanna, gives them too much value, and struggles to understand universal laws or karma. Similarly, if one happens to appreciate merely socially created monks and nuns with an underlying tendency to think they represent noble Sangha, but if they happen to mistakenly ignore universally created noble Sangha, the Sotapanna state cannot be experienced. This is because when someone gives too much value to the socially constructed Triple Gem, they may mistakenly ignore the true Triple Gem, which can impact their ability to shape universal energies and karma. Thus, one may take extra care when they come to practice Dhamma, practicing in the way it should be, considering the universal laws and rhythms.

In terms of a practice, to letting go of self-view, when you think of something as belonging to you, along with an underlying tendency to consider it stable, understand that it can lead to worry and fear about losing it. Also, an excessive need to protect what you perceive as yours with an underlying tendency to consider it stable can make you feel weary. Instead, if you recognize that things are not stable but focus on making the most of each moment of your life, you can ease the burden on your mind.

Applying wisdom can help alleviate extreme sadness and worry during challenging situations. When you face various difficulties and encounter many problems in life, if you can focus your energy on actively resolving them without expecting everything to happen as you wish, you can conserve the energy needed to address the challenges you encounter daily while keeping excessive worries down. This is how you can practice letting go of mental attachment or "renouncing the world through sensory information" on the universal noble path.

If you were to engage in practice meditation as a separate activity, that's not sufficient. Instead, you need to apply Dhamma within daily activities, in a way that allows you to experience peace and happiness in life. To do that, you may focus on reducing grasping self-view and conventions including social practices in mind within your daily life. In addition to the practice of letting go of grasping, "self-view," and conventions, and may also consider letting go of doubts while connecting with and developing friendships with those who embody the four stages of nibbana. Among spiritual friends, there are likely to be those who are genuine and who truly want to practice in accordance with the universal Buddha and universal Dhamma. It is for their benefit, with care and compassion, that teachings of the Buddha related to the fetters and universal Triple Gem are revealed, especially because four stages of nibbana, fetters and the Triple Gem are interconnected and not separate.

Bear in mind that understanding universal noble truths can be difficult if you become too attached to social frameworks or mental constructs. For example, if you consider nibbana as merely a "religion' or 'tradition" or "lifestyle", you'll find that your understanding is limited to that framework. If you cling to these mental frames, you will struggle to see beyond them. Instead, if you keep space to discover new things, that will aid broaden your understanding to discover universal truth. Based on pre-existing beliefs, some spiritual friends may think that ordinary monks are well-versed in the Dhamma. They may receive protection and recognition from society but such things are temporary. Since these individuals have not experienced the Dhamma, they lack true protection from nibbana or samsara. Yet, all spiritual friends can learn beyond the social frameworks and apply the Dhamma within themselves to receive protection by practicing letting go of the fetters that bind them to delusion in daily life.

Chapter 30
Noble meditation practice

Dhamma is a self-practice. Thus, you may hear about the practice and apply it to yourself to discover yourself during your usual activities.

Engaging in noble meditation can help you experience nibbana or Sotapanna. You may build up noble meditation practice based on what you already know. Mindfulness, commonly practiced, asks you to focus on what you are sensing and feeling at the moment without being overly reactive. Whenever you bring awareness to what you are experiencing or to your state of mind via your thoughts, you are being mindful. To move into the next level of, you may choose to apply wisdom and focus on your thoughts when you experience discomfort or distress in daily life. Reflect on how distress is a part of life and understand that whenever you have likes or dislikes for earthly or worldly experiences, distress arises as they change. This is the nature of life. Life is short, so making the best of it is wise. Instead of worrying excessively, it is more beneficial to focus your attention on resolving issues. If you are fond of meditations, strive to make your life a noble meditation—a place where you apply wisdom and noble qualities day and night.

The reason why all spiritual friends in monasteries and homes do not experience the fourfold nibbana is simply because they are not understanding, following, or practicing in line with the words of the Buddha. Now that universal Dhamma, path to Sotapanna is revealed to you, you may test the practice.

Chapter 31
Universe within

You are a part of the universe, and the universe is within you. When you try to understand the functioning of the Earth, gravity, stars, volcanoes, winds, and so on, a person tends to think they are trying to understand the functioning of nature that is happening within the universe from the outside self. Whatever happen outside is produced within.

The world is experienced within. A person cannot see one's own face without a mirror, and in the same way a person cannot see outside without the kind of mirror effects of an outside produced within. It's more like the universe creating mirror images of an outside within inside a person, a cosmic illusion created in an illusion of a self. Every person, while being connected with both the universe and society, experiences conventional understanding of self. Middleway means you don't run away from the universe but live as usual, and you don't run away from society but continue to live in your usual ways; you merely understand universal nature within you with wisdom while alive, so that you don't get deluded, or you don't take worldly experiences as too much important, instead you let them go at ease by applying wisdom.

Given the uncertainty of worldly experiences, if you think taking in and developing expectations for worldly experience is important and precious, you develop delusion. Given the uncertainty of life, if you think it is not worth the pain of touching the world too much in mind, and thus, making each moment the wise thing to do, you let go of delusion. If you were to continue letting go of delusions through wisdom, you could prolong letting go of suffering.

When you grasp your experiences in an unwise or deluded way—or when you think that everything you expect should happen, that you should always get what you like and avoid what you dislike, and that people you favor should always be there for you—you set yourself up for distress if those expectations are not met. Instead, understand that things you expect may not always happen, and that both likes and dislikes may occur from time to time. At times, people you expect to care for you may let you down, and such experiences can be a part of life. Understand that it is not wise to make such experiences a big deal or a reason to suffer in mind, and instead focus more on resolving things that need resolving to make the most of each moment. Focus on finding peace within and develop wholesome mind states. Wholesome means you do not hurt yourself or others. This can be achieved by shifting your focus away from what others do or do not do. Instead, focus on yourself. Do your best to resolve things and fulfill your obligations to others. Strive to be someone who does not rely on unkind social practices that divide people. Let go of pride grounded on delusion. Let go of excessive likes or dislikes driven by delusion, ill will, or the need to compare people. Engage in activities you choose and choose wholesome ones that benefit yourself or others. Maintain wholesome intentions day and night. Try to share what you have with others rather than just consume for yourself. Let go of delusion at any time to let go of inner fires within.

The nature of the universe is that worldly experiences are subject to change, and when you give too much value to worldly experiences, grounding delusion, they can make you suffer a lot as you continue to touch mind such made experiences again and again. Instead, if you train your mind to give value to renouncing worldly experiences, meaning letting go of lack of wisdom, your sufferings will cease even for a moment when you apply the wisdom, but wisdom will not stay stable until you experience Sotapanna. Thus, you may combine conscious efforts to grow in wisdom while linking with the Triple Gem in your mental continuum to experience Sotapanna.

Understand that when you give too much importance to worldly experiences based on sensory information, given the changing nature that make up ups and downs of worldly experience; what you give too much value or importance can make you suffer. Thus, every time a person gives too much importance to their worldly experiences, regardless of their conventional background, the same things they value through worldly experience can produce suffering.

Understand that delusion is in your thinking, you can think with wisdom, or you can think with delusion. If you were to think that someone you like or trust always should be there for you, and when expectations fail, you can suffer. Instead, if you were to think that anything is possible in the world, I would just do my part and fulfil my responsibilities and find peace within myself. You are likely to experience peace by relying on yourself, that is, training to let go of delusions or unwholesome thoughts within you. In this manner, if you continue to train your mind and make yourself a person, you can rely on finding happiness and peace by applying wisdom, which is a way of delving into the wisdom-based noble path.

On the path to Sotapanna, you have your mind to experience and understand with wisdom, but there are no Buddhist temples, flags, robes, or ritualistic attire; it's a process of understanding the nature of the self, or the emptiness of a stable self, through wisdom within.

Nibbana addresses human nature. Human beings inherently have needs, some of which are basic. These include food to satisfy hunger, water to quench thirst, and the pursuit of happiness and peace from worldly distress in daily life—

experiences they can enjoy while alive, without having to wait until after death or step outside their usual routine activities. Nibbana offers an escape from worldly distress and mental suffering, allowing individuals to find relief within their daily routines while still alive. This understanding reflects the perfect quality of the Buddha's universal Dhamma.

Nature is designed in such a way that food can satisfy hunger temporary, but it does not eliminate the need to eat again, and water can quench thirst only for a short time before the need arises again. Meditation practices, jhanas, conventional lifestyles, and various other techniques can provide temporary relief from mental distress without addressing the root causes of suffering. As a result, the need to seek happiness and peace arises again for those who do not possess such qualities. Yet, having previously experienced limitless happiness as a Sotapanna, and having felt incomparable joy and peace as an Anagami, an Arahant becomes free from desires after having experienced the best of the world. Once you have experienced the best, you do not seek anything more, and that is human nature. This is how nibbana a is designed to address human needs and nature, in accordance with Dhamma niyama.

> "When he was seated to one side, Arahant Sāriputta said to the Blessed One, "Venerable Sir, this line ofthought arose in my mind when I was alone in

> solitude: 'For which Buddhas did the Holy Life last a long time?'.."
>
> "Venerable Sir, what is the cause, what is the condition because of which the Holy Life did not last a long time for the Blessed One Vipassī, the Blessed One Sikhī, and the Blessed One Vessabhū?"
>
> "Sāriputta, the Blessed One Vipassī, the Blessed One Sikhī, and the Blessed One Vessabhū were hesitant to teach the Dhamma in detail to their outsider disciples. They taught few discourses, poems, explanations, stanzas, utterances, quotations, birth-stories, marvels, and catechisms. Preliminary training-rules were not designated for their ordinary disciples in monasteries. The Pātimokkha was not recited. When those Buddhas, those Blessed Ones disappeared, and the noble disciples who had awakened across four stages of nibbana along with those Buddha disappeared, the subsequent ordinary disciples of various names, clans, lineages, and families who had gone forth quickly caused that Holy Life to disappear."-The Mahā-Vibhaṅga from the Vinaya

To a great extent, an ordinary disciple can make Sotapanna and nibbana disappear. Noble disciple makes Sotapanna and nibbana appear.

Typically, in the absence of the Buddha and Arahants, universal Dhamma does not come alive, but preliminary Dhamma continues to exist over centuries. Conventional Dhamma serves as the foundation, as with preliminary Dhamma, it becomes easier to share higher teachings of the

Buddha. When Arahants are present, the Dhamma remains vital. You may link preliminary Dhamma practices to the universal training path to Sotapanna by expanding and growing your practice in line with the noble view to experience Sotapanna.

To summarize: what is the practice leading to Sotapanna? It involves renouncing likes, dislikes, and expectations within daily life, meaning letting go of self-view. One should also refrain from treating people differently based on conventions and avoid grasping conventions, build spiritual friendships with Arahants while engaging in wholesome deeds.

Emptiness is in the nature. The universe operates under certain laws and order. By nature, the universally applicable Triple Gem are empty in delusion, and are empty in generating fuel within. Nibbana is inherently found in nature. Thus, reflecting on the qualities of the universal Buddha, the universal Dhamma, and the universal Sangha is essential for purifying thoughts from grasping fetters and for maintaining noble virtues in your daily life. This practice is applicable to everyone.

Web sources

Dhammatalks.org. https://www.dhammatalks.org

SuttaCentral.net. https://suttacentral.net

Tripitaka.net. https://www.tipitaka.net/tipitaka/dhp/

Research papers:

Glück, J., Bluck, S. & Weststrate, N.M. More on the MORE Life Experience Model: What We Have Learned (So Far). *J Value Inquiry* 53, 349–370 (2019).

Weststrate, Nic. (2019). The Mirror of Wisdom: Self-Reflection as a Developmental Precursor and Core Competency of Wise People. 10.1017/9781108568272.024.

Images

intueri/shutterstock.com

alliesu 5/shutterstock.com

Chittagong Hill Tract/shutterstock.com